Notable Women
of
Victorian Hastings

A COLLECTION OF
MINI-BIOGRAPHIES

HELENA WOJTCZAK

Published by
THE HASTINGS PRESS
PO Box 96 Hastings TN34 1GQ
hastings.press@virgin.net
www. hastingspress.co.uk

by the same author:
Women of Victorian Hastings - ISBN 1 904 109 02 0
Down & Out in Victorian Hastings - ISBN 1 904 109 01 2

Set in Times New Roman 10 bold.

Cover illustration: an oil painting of Dr. Elizabeth Blackwell M.D. by Joseph Stanley Kozlowski, 1963.

Printed and bound by Antony Rowe Ltd, Eastbourne.

ABOUT THE AUTHOR

Helena Wojtczak BSc (Hons) was born in Sussex and raised in London. She has worked on the railways, in administration and as a musicians' agent. After graduating in psychology she undertook three years' postgraduate study in social, women's, and oral history. As Consultant Historian to the National Railway Museum, York, she co-produced a major exhibition on railway workers in 1996-7. In 1998 St Mary-in-the-Castle Arts Centre, Hastings, displayed her work on the suffrage movement, and in 2002 she produced an exhibition for Hastings Museum on Victorian Women of Hastings. Helena has produced two award-winning history websites: *Railway Women in Wartime* and *Women of Hastings & St Leonards* and has contributed to several others including *The Victorian Web* and *Encyclopedia Titanica*. She has been featured in newspapers and has appeared on television and radio, and has been published by the Oxford University Press and by the Railway Ancestors Family History Society. Helena currently lives in St Leonards and is writing a book on railway labour history.

CONTENTS

INTRODUCTION

Most informed residents of Hastings can reel off a list of notable Victorian men connected to the town: Coventry Patmore, Grey Owl, George Macdonald, Robert Tressell. But what of the women? Cannot Hastings boast some ladies who have distinguished themselves in some way? It most certainly can; they have simply been overlooked or disregarded and it is time they were given the acclaim they deserve.

The organised women's rights movement in Britain was begun in the 1850s by Barbara Bodichon and Bessie Rayner Parkes. Lady Annie Brassey was the first woman to circumnavigate the globe. Marianne North was the first woman botanical painter. Elizabeth Blackwell and Sophia Jex-Blake opened the field of medicine to women. Edith Chubb was the first woman Bachelor of Music, and Matilda Betham Edwards was the first English woman to be made an Officier De L'Instruction Publique de France. Elsie Bowerman was the first female barrister to address the Old Bailey, and the first woman president of the United Nations Committee on the Status of Women.

Barbara Bodichon links all these women. Four of them knew her personally, but the other four are connected to her by curious coincidences. Bodichon and North were both painters whose fathers were MPs. Bodichon co-founded the women's suffrage movement and Girton College; fifty years later Elsie Bowerman was a suffragette who attended Girton. After Lady Brassey's death, her husband attended women's rights meetings with Bodichon and donated money to Girton; Edith Chubb lived above the shop in which Bodichon's petition had been held fifty years previously.

None of these short biographies claims to be comprehensive; they offer an introduction in bite-sized pieces to whet the reader's appetite and to place some notable women firmly in the annals of Hastings history.

My thanks are due to the staff of Hastings Reference Library, to Eric Bond Hutton, and to Cameron Moffett.

Helena Wojtczak, April 2002

MARIANNE NORTH
Botanical Painter
1830-1890

arianne North was born at Hastings Lodge, Old London Road - now the site of Marianne Park, a recent housing development. Her family was one of the richest, best-connected and most prestigious in town. Her father Frederick was a wealthy magistrate and was Mayor of Hastings in 1826, 28 and 30 and its MP in 1831-37, 54-64, and 68.[1] His aunt was Sarah, the Countess Waldegrave, Hastings' chief benefactress of the Victorian age.[2] Marianne had a half-sister, Janet, from her mother's first marriage to Sir John Marjoribanks, a Baronet; an elder brother, Charles, and a younger sister, Catherine. Among the family's acquaintance were many artistic and literary figures, including Samuel Prout, William Hunt, Edward Lear, George Bentham, Lady Duff Gordon and Charles Darwin.

Marianne was educated at home by a local governess, Maria Wenham. She was also trained to sing, and a Dutchwoman - Miss van Fowinkel - taught her flower-painting. These kinds of artistic endeavours were acceptable for women only as 'accomplishments' because it was considered unbecoming for a lady to aspire to a profession and immodest to have her name displayed in public places.

The Norths spent a lot of their time travelling: even the yearly journey to the family estates in Norfolk took a week by horse-carriage. They spent almost three years touring Europe, sketching and painting everywhere they went. After Marianne's mother died in 1855, North and his daughters continued to travel when Parliament was in recess and in the years that he failed to be elected as MP.

In 1864 Catherine married John Addington Symonds[3] at St Clement's Church. Soon afterwards, North lost his seat as MP. He let Hastings Lodge and travelled with Marianne to Switzerland, Austria, Egypt and Syria. The pair spent most of 1867-8 in Hastings, where a Christmas house-guest, the artist Robert Dowling, taught Marianne to paint in oils. North regained his parliamentary seat in the 1867 general election; however, the following year was taken ill abroad and Marianne brought him home, where he died in 1869. He was buried in Halton Churchyard. Marianne had been devoted to her father and was inconsolable.

With her large inheritance and handsome face, suitors would have been abundant, had she chosen to marry, but she remained mistress of her

HASTINGS LODGE, SUSSEX.

TO BE LET, UNFURNISHED

A HANDSOME DETACHED RESIDENCE, About a mile and a half from Hastings Railway Station, known as HASTINGS LODGE . Lately occupied by F. North, ESQ, M.P., deceased. It is in a high situation, and commands CHARMING LAND AND SEA VIEWS Is in thorough repair, and contains 13 bedrooms, dressing and fitted bath rooms, splendid drawing and dining rooms, opening to verandah, with sea view ; Establishment : capital stabling for four horses, coach house, harness room, and five rooms for men servants, &c, with grounds of between three and four acres, which are well-timbered affording considerable seclusion, and include level croquet lawns, shrubberies, shaded walks, sloping lawns, a small paddock, and productive kitchen garden, with vinery and potting house, &c.

For further particulars apply at the offices of
JAMES COLEMAN VIDLER,
Auctioneer, Land, House, & Estate Agent
16, Havelock Road, Hastings

A newspaper advertisement from 1871 to let Hastings Lodge, Marianne's home for 41 years until she set off alone for a trip to Boston and never lived there again.

When a family home the house was the venue for many grand balls and dinner parties, to which were invited all the local gentry and nobility. The house had extensive and beautiful gardens, in which Marianne served her apprenticeship as an artist by cultivating and painting flowers and plants.

The house no longer stands. The site, near the corner of Ashburnham Road, was used firstly for a sanatorium and later for a convent and Sacred Heart School. This has now been developed into private housing and is called *Marianne Park*.

own destiny and fortune. Labelling marriage 'a terrible experiment', she once commented that she 'preferred vegetables to the settled domestic life'.[4]

In 1871 she forsook Hastings society, let the Lodge and left Hastings forever. At the invitation of a rich Boston widow she had once met on a Nile cruise, she sailed to the USA from Liverpool on the Cunard steamer *Malta*. However, Marianne soon wearied of Boston high society and came to realise that her true desire was to travel alone and to meet all kinds of people, not just the wealthy. She went to Jamaica and Brazil, where she painted exotic flora in oils. Her second trip, of two years' duration, began with a few months at Tenerife in 1875 and took in San Francisco, Yosemite, Japan, Borneo, Java, and Ceylon, where she met the famous photographer and fellow lady traveller, Mrs. Julia Margaret Cameron. Marianne found Anglo-Indian society tedious, and could not wait to escape to a natural environment. She travelled to the Himalayas, despite suffering badly from rheumatism in the cold weather.

In 1877 her sketches were exhibited in London and she was thrilled when the Emperor of Brazil asked to see her paintings, which at that time were housed in her London flat near Victoria Station. News of her work had reached Hastings, where the local newspaper remarked that she had 'long been known to the scientific world as a distinguished amateur and an indefatigable traveller'. She spent 1878 in India and, on her return, hired a gallery to exhibit her oil paintings. She wrote to Sir Joseph Hooker, Director of the Royal Botanical Society, offering to pay for a special gallery at Kew Gardens where her work could be permanently housed. According to notes made in a private scrapbook by the editor of the *Hastings & St Leonards Times*, 'her paintings are still exhibited at Kew because Hastings could not find a place for them.'[5]

Marianne's work is of great botanical importance because she depicted nature as she saw it, using oil paints as a modern-day botanist would use close-up photography. She endeavoured to capture every detail, every vivid colour. The result, as can be seen on page 15 and on the rear cover of this book, is lucid, resplendent and intense. She painted the backgrounds and landscapes, placing the flora in their natural context. Her methods were unorthodox: she squeezed paint straight from the tube, sketched on the move and, on arrival at seaports, posted her pictures to Kew for safe-keeping. She collected plant cuttings in an old tin filled with wet sand.

Marianne had one genus and four species named after her. Four of them were first recorded by her:

Northea seychellana - a tree in the Seychelles, a previously unreported genus.
Nepenthes northiana - the large pitcher plant of Borneo, first painted by her.
Crinum northianum - one of the Amaryllis relatives.
Areca northiana - one of the feather palms.
Kniphofia northiana - one of the African torch lilies or poker plants.

Above Marianne North in 1868, sketching on Elephantine Island. *Drawing a Friendly Audience* by Phené Spiers. *Below* Marianne photographed at her easel in a distant jungle.

Marianne was more than a painter. Her journal, *Recollections of a Happy Life,* is pure joy to read; not only for the delightful and evocative descriptions of plants, flowers, insects, birds and landscapes but as an historical document of 19th-century travel and living conditions across the world. Some of her pen-sketches of people she met are cruelly comical, like this one, written in Brazil:

> Another cold day's ride brought us to a large farmhouse belonging to a very remarkable family, who would have made their fortunes at fairs. The farmer himself was perfectly round, with a bullet head and face, all over which grew hair and beard apparently cut with his wife's bluntest pair of scissors as close as he could with his left hand. His fat wife had a thick black beard and moustache (uncut), her grandmother the same in gray, The children were all perfectly round, like their fascinating parents, but as yet beardless.

Marianne travelled to six continents, an extraordinary feat bearing in mind the irregularity, slowness and discomfort of travel in Victorian times. After long steam-ship voyages, she travelled in horse-drawn carriages, ox- and bullock-carts, in canoes, on horseback, and by foot along dirt-track roads and jungle tracks. She was truly an intrepid, daring and determined woman. A writer for the *Los Angeles Times* pointed out that,

> At the age of 53, she climbed on a pile of boulders to paint the exotic coco de mer, a tall palm with a gigantic nut, endemic to the Seychelles. … When North's search for flowering specimens took her off the beaten path, she bedded down in barns or by campfires and never flinched when, for instance, a servant in Borneo sliced leeches off her legs with a long sword.[6]

Once she had experienced the excitement and freedom of world-wide travel as a woman alone, Marianne could not return to the narrowly restrictive and shallow high-society life she had eschewed. She went home to England only to regain strength, to see to her financial affairs and to gather fresh supplies of painting materials for her next expedition. At Darwin's suggestion she went to Australia and New Zealand in 1880, returning via Honolulu to the USA, which she crossed by train, then she sailed back to Liverpool.

In 1881-2 she undertook all the preparations for the gallery at Kew, supervised the architect, and painted the frieze and decorations around the doors. She then began to feel dissatisfied that Africa was not represented and so, despite poor health, rheumatism and encroaching deafness, she travelled there in 1882. In 1883 she returned to London, organised an extension to the gallery then set out again, this time for the Seychelles where her nerves 'broke down from insufficient food and overwork'. Despite that, she went to Chile in 1884 where, in only four months she created 32 oil paintings, inspired by the Araucarias and fauna. She then planned a trip to Mexico; however, she was too tired and too ill to travel.

Marianne's attitude to wealth is revealed in this passage from *Recollections*:

> [In Grahamstown] three girls forced themselves into my room … and began asking me stupid questions till I fairly lost my temper. "Was I not afraid of spoiling my eyes? I ought to save them." I asked her in return what eyes were made for, and did she think it would be any use to leave them behind me? Like her beloved diamonds or gold, what good would it do to save them?

Marianne is not without her critics, mainly politically-correct, female American academics. She has been roundly castigated for using racist terminology while describing indigenous people, though it seems to be asking rather a lot to expect just one woman to be completely different in this respect from her peer group and from the society in which she was raised. Suchitra Mathur[7] called her writings 'the female version of male imperialist rhetoric'. Susan Morgan, in her introduction to the 1993 American edition of *Recollections,* **sees North as 'one of the boys' rather than as a feminist. She criticised Marianne's comments about contented Brazilian slaves and the '4½ -foot-high' Japanese governor of Kyoto. But it was Marianne's style to make comical, even caustic, comments about anyone she met, of any colour or race: she once remarked 'What a killing race the British are!'[8] and at one point records that the native servants were making fun of her:**

> She had the queerest collection of servants there, and some little creatures to wait at the table who were black as coals, full of fun and games behind the door. They were great mimics, and took off all our peculiarities behind our backs. I caught one of them pretending to paint in a pair of straw spectacles, with a bit of white rag on its head like my cap, and cross-sticks for an easel, the others roaring with laughter.

Morgan also disapproves that Marianne 'wields the privileges of her upper-class background to adopt the more masculine role of the independent naturalist'.[9] Similarly, Julia Gergits[10] wrote:

> The [North Gallery] and its contents truly are... expressions of a controlling vision that converted native flora and fauna into images arranged and depicted to satisfy the imperial imagination... North benefited from the administrative machinery of British imperialism … Wherever she went, she enjoyed the privileges of being not only a British citizen but of having what amounted to diplomatic connections... she scarcely mentions the indigenous peoples of the areas through which she travels. Society, when mentioned at all, is always British society. When she painted a scene, she either erased the native presence or pictorialized it in ways that reflected her position as a privileged viewer.

It is true that Marianne was well-connected. She carried with her letters of introduction and she sometimes she accepted hospitality from colonial statesmen and English-speaking dignitaries: indeed, on arrival at Wellington, she stayed with the Premier of New Zealand and in the USA she was the guest of President Grant at the White House. However, Marianne also stayed with people in modest circumstances and was prepared to accept with grace whatever accommodation she was offered. She sometimes slept, without complaint, on verandahs or in dilapidated barns devoid of the facilities to which, in her privileged upbringing, she was accustomed. In Brazil she did most of her work in a hut in the jungle. Of her accommodation in South Africa, she wrote:

I was taken across a sort of drawbridge to an attic or wide verandah, dark with a solid mass of creepers, bougainvillea, banksia-roses, etc. It was full of old boxes of rubbish, and some crazy steps led into another attic with a small room at either end, one of them given up entirely to a colony of bees, which had built in a corner and resisted intruders...There I settled myself, digging out a hole in the bougainvilleas, which let in a blaze of rosy light through their flowery wreaths.

One side of the room was separated from the verandah by broken green-house sashes, one of them off its hinges. The roof itself was all of a slant, books, hats, pipes, and various treasures of men in delightful disorder, but it was deliciously quiet and out of the way. I bolted myself in at night, and shared the whole storey with the bees and an occasional rat, bird, or lizard...

My hut was water-tight, and very comfortable, except for the abundant mosquitoes (who bit by day instead of by night there),and the rats woke one up at night, often close to one's head. One night there was a terrible noise; something hard was banging about, knocking the metal bath and wooden boxes all round. I saw something long in the moonlight moving over the floor. Flying to the door, I set it wide open. All was still outside. I sprang on my bed, lit my candle, and poked at the thing with a long Kafir spear, hoping it would go out. It rushed under my bed, and I saw it was a rat, only a rat, jumping frantically, which quieted my worst fears; so I put out my light again and slept. In the morning I found a horrid trap had been set (unknown to me). The poor thing's leg had been broken by it, and he had escaped on three. Some days after there was a fearful smell. We could find the dead body nowhere, so I had to go into the sitting-room-hut till the ants had cleared it away.

It seems harsh to condemn Marianne for accepting invitations to stay in civilised comfort with English speaking people, and unfair to cite only the luxury moments while overlooking the hardships encountered during more than a decade of world-wide travel. At the age of 53 Marianne was in South Africa when, after 'a six hours' jolt-jolt to Port Alfred' with a female friend she found that,

Our stupid driver put us down at the wrong hotel, from which we had to walk down the hill to the Kowie River to be ferried across, then had a hot mile's walk across the wet marsh and up the opposite hill to the other, where rooms had been taken for us, carrying all our luggage ourselves in the hottest hours of a hot day!

More than once she overturned a dilapidated cart into a ford or river, and was soaked to her skin with mud. Her journal describes how she scaled cliffs and crossed swampland to reach the plants she sought, with little regard for her own safety. This and much more decidedly unladylike behaviour shows Marianne's true personality.

We got a fresh carriage at the station, and some bread and cheese. Mrs. M. borrowed a shawl, and we started, floundering through swamps, bogs, and swollen rivers for an hour and a half, till at last we reached the road over Baines Kloof... Most of the flowers were over but the wild scene was worth the trouble of going.

Marianne completed 848 oil paintings in 13 years, of which 832 were given to Kew Gardens and displayed in the North Gallery. The Gallery is unusual because it contains almost the entire body of work of one artist, and because the paintings cover every inch of wall-space. In addition, the dado panels are made of 246 different types of wood, from six continents, all collected by Marianne.

The public opening of the Gallery was a huge success. In 1884 Marianne received a letter from Queen Victoria's Private Secretary. He stated that, having been told by her ministers that there was no equivalent accolade to a knighthood for women, the Queen wished somehow to give Marianne public recognition for her generosity for the gift to the nation of the North Gallery. Instead of a knighthood, Marianne received a signed photograph of Her Majesty.

In January 1885 Marianne rented an idyllic cottage with gardens in Alderley, Gloucestershire. In October she spent a few days with her Aunt Arabella at The Croft, Croft Road, from where she saw all her old Hastings friends and acquaintances. The *Hastings & St Leonards News* remarked, rather curiously: 'Her long journeys are now probably over, and she is likely to settle down in London to useful work.'[11] Being in poor health, she asked Sir Joseph Hooker to negotiate with Macmillan to publish her journal. But the manuscript was overlong, and Marianne was too ill to shorten it. After Marianne's death in 1890 her sister Catherine edited and published the journal as *Recollections of a Happy Life* in 1892 and *Further Recollections of a Happy Life* the following year.

Marianne North's paintings constitute a considerable botanical achievement. Many of the plants depicted are endangered species, some are already extinct. The paintings remain in their original cheek-by-jowl arrangement in the Gallery, which has been described as 'a precious, jewel-

encrusted box'. It is one of the most popular attractions at Kew Gardens. American journalist Bud Collins wrote that the two rooms of the Gallery

are a shrine to North, the walls solidly covered with her vivid oils ... It took her a year just to arrange them as a dazzling display in many colors - blossoms, billowing trees, landscapes ... "In your face!'" is an expression that she wouldn't have used. But it fits as she bowls you over with her life's work - blooming, thriving, some of it indestructible like her Niagara Falls, or the Atlantic crashing against rocks at Manchester-by-the-Sea, Mass. Kangaroos and koalas. The Taj Mahal. Ostriches hatching jumbo eggs. What a cast of flora and fauna.[12]

In 1983 the Seychelles issued a series of stamps depicting four of Marianne's paintings, to commemorate the centennial of Marianne's visit. In 2000 an exhibition of her Chilean paintings opened at the Museo Histórico Nacional, Santiago, after which it toured the whole country. Kew Gardens sells a range of Marianne North merchandise including jigsaws, calendars and playing cards. Marianne is a popular subject for articles, talks and lectures, including one at Hastings Museum in 2001.

Marianne is not generally labelled a feminist, unlike fellow painter Barbara Bodichon. This is because she was not involved with the organised women's movement. And yet Marianne lived her life by feminist principles; she achieved personal liberation by simply ignoring the restrictions placed upon Victorian women. She made many deliberate choices: to remain single, to spend her inheritance on her career, to ignore what society expected of her as a well-brought up lady. Travelling across the world as a spinster was daring enough, but Marianne also threw aside established standards of Victorian femininity, tramping through jungles, shortening her petticoats, sewing bank-notes into her dresses, wearing workaday clothes and sturdy boots which were soon shabby from rough usage. She developed hefty biceps from carrying her own easel and materials, and allowed the rays of the tropical sun to bronze her, against the contemporary doctrine that skin must be white to be 'ladylike'. She chose freedom not only from a husband but from the suffocating social restrictions of women at that time. Marianne did exactly what she wanted.

FURTHER READING

Recollections of a Happy Life: Being the Autobiography of Marianne North. (1892) Ed. Catherine North Symonds. 2 vols. London and New York: Macmillan.

Some Further Recollections of a Happy Life, Selected from the Journals of Marianne North, Chiefly Between the Years 1859 and 1869. (1893) Ed. Catherine North Symonds. London and New York: Macmillan.

A Vision of Eden: The Life and Work of Marianne North. Webb & Bower (1980). Abridged text of *Recollections* plus biographical notes, introductions, etc. Fully illustrated with many colour plates of Marianne's paintings.

Middleton, D. (1965) *Victorian Lady Travellers.* Routledge & Kegan Paul.
O'Conner, M. *Marianne North. British Travel Writers, 1876-1909.* Eds. Barbara Brothers and Julia Gergits. Detroit: Gale Research, 1997. 251-255.

REFERENCES

[1] A Town Commissioner, he chaired the great inaugural banquet to celebrate the opening of the new town of St Leonards on 28th October 1829. He was immensely popular: when first elected MP he gained 38% of the votes and at his final election, 37 years later, 51% chose him

[2] A short biography of the Countess appears in Wojtczak, H. (2002) *Women of Victorian Hastings.* The Hastings Press.

[3] John Addington Symonds, art critic, historian and homosexual. The couple had four children but, inevitably, were soon leading separate lives. Once her children were grown Catherine, effectively a widow but unable to remarry, turned her attentions to editing and publishing Marianne's writings.

[4] *Los Angeles Times,* 29 July 2001

[5] This scrapbook is held at Hastings Reference Library. Decimus Burton, son of the founder of St Leonards, designed both the Temperate House and the Palm House at Kew.

[6] *Los Angeles Times,* 29 July 2001

[7] Wayne State University.

[8] *Los Angeles Times,* 29 July 2001

[9] Morgan, S. *Place Matters: Gendered Geography in Victorian Women's Travel Books about Southeast Asia* . New Brunswick, NJ: Rutgers University Press, 1996.

[10] Youngstown State University.

[11] *Hastings & St Leonards News,* 9 Oct 1885

[12] *Boston Globe,* 26 August 2001.

KEY TO PHOTOGRAPHS

Paintings by Marianne North

 Page 15

Top left:	*The tomb of Ala ud Din*, Delhi, India.
Top right:	*Nest of the Trabajor Lessor Canestero*, in Chile.
Middle left:	*Nepenthes Rafflesiana*, the Pitcher plant.
Middle centre:	*Nepenthes.*
Middle right:	*Nepenthes Northiana*, Borneo.
Below left:	*Casa.*
Below middle:	*Coral Tree*, Brazil.
Below right:	*Poinsettia* or *Christmas Flower*, Morro Velho, Brazil.

Photographs reproduced courtesy of the Royal Botanical Society.

Paintings by Barbara Leigh Smith Bodichon

 Page 16

Top:	*At Ventnor, Isle of Wight*, watercolour, 1856.
Middle left:	*Algerian study*, watercolour.
Middle right:	*Study of Sunflowers*, oil on canvas.
Below:	*Sisters Working in our Fields*, Algeria, c. 1858-60. The scene is from the 'villa on the green heights of Mustapha Superieur, commanding a glorious view of sea, city and plain.'

Study of Sunflowers is reproduced courtesy of Girton College, Cambridge.

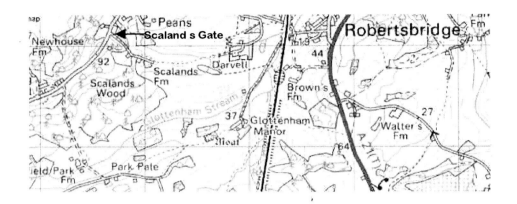

Contemporary map showing the location of Barbara's childhood home, Brown's Farm, her brothers' land at Glottenham Manor and Scalands Farm, and the house she commissioned in 1863, Scaland's Gate. Barbara's many illustrious and famous guests travelled by train to Robertsbridge and thence by horse-drawn carriage. She died there in 1891, and was buried at nearby Brightling. *Below* Brown's Farm in 1998.

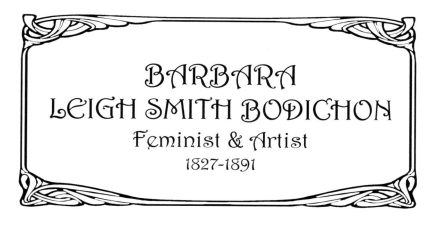

BARBARA LEIGH SMITH BODICHON
Feminist & Artist
1827-1891

'I hope there are some who will brave ridicule for the sake of common justice to half the people in the world'.

Barbara Bodichon

arbara Leigh Smith was born in Whatlington, near Battle,[1] on 11th April 1827. She was an extraordinary, unconventional woman and a free spirit, who eschewed high society and despite her wealth allied herself with the bohemian, the artistic and the downtrodden. She spurned chaperones, and startled respectable society - even, at times, her own friends. All of her 'extremist' feminist ideas are now entrenched in our current laws and beliefs. Barbara's name has been little heard until recently, in sharp contrast to some of her contemporaries who achieved less or whose breadth of interest was narrower.[2] Barbara is, arguably, the most effective 'mover and shaker' to emerge from Victorian Hastings.

Her father's residence was 5 Blandford Square, Marylebone, London. From 1816 onward he inherited and purchased property in Sussex: Brown's Farm near Robertsbridge, with a house built about 1700 (extant), and Crowham Manor, Westfield, with 200 acres. During the 1840s Smith bought more land to the south and west of Robertsbridge, including Scalands Farm (extant), Mountfield Park Farm (extant) and Glottenham Manor (rebuilt and now a nursing home).

Smith was a man of radical views, a Dissenter, a Unitarian, a supporter of Free Trade and a benefactor to the poor. In 1826 he bore the cost of building a school for the inner city poor at Vincent Square, Westminster, and paid half the fees for each child. His niece (his sister's daughter) was Florence Nightingale, and his father wanted him to marry a girl in the Nightingale family, but in Derbyshire in 1826 Smith met Anne Longden, a 25-year-old milliner. She became pregnant and Smith took her to a rented lodge in the village of Whatlington, near Battle. There she lived

PELHAM CRESCENT, HASTINGS:
BARBARA LEIGH SMITH'S HOME FOR 17 YEARS.
Above Pelham Crescent as it looked when the Smiths moved there in the 1830s. Theirs was the second house to the left of St Mary's Chapel. Barbara's friend and sister feminist Bessie Rayner Parkes lived for a short time at no 6, two doors to the right of the chapel. *Below* the Crescent c1860s. It was recently reported that Pelham Crescent is among the top 6% most architecturally-important buildings in the UK, so, hopefully, its survival is guaranteed.

as 'Mrs Leigh', the surname of Smith's relations on the Isle of Wight. The child, Barbara, was born on 8 April 1827. Smith rode on horseback from Brown's Farm to visit them daily, and within eight weeks Anne was pregnant again. When Ben junior was born they went to America for two years and on their return lived openly together at Brown's, where they had two more children. In 1833, Anne became ill and Smith took her to a seafront house: 9 Pelham Crescent; the health-giving properties of Hastings' sea-air were highly regarded at the time. A local woman, Hannah Walker, was employed to look after the children. Anne's illness became worse. Smith took her to Ryde, Isle of Wight, where she died, in 1834.

It is something of a mystery that the couple never wed. The scandal of marrying a woman from a lower social class was as nothing compared with raising five children out of wedlock. Biographer Pam Hirsch suggests that Smith did not want Anne and the children to become his chattels.

In 1836 Smith was elected MP for Norwich. Aunts Dolly Longden or Julia Smith tended the children and Smith engaged Catherine Spooner as governess and Harry Porter as Latin and history tutor. Their riding master, Mr William Willetts, was the foremost in Hastings. Despite having illegitimate children, Benjamin Smith maintained his social respectability and became a magistrate in Hastings in 1845.

Smith was by all accounts a loving and attentive father who adored his children and who took them out and about. In 1838 the local press mentioned that he took them to the Hastings horse-races [3] and in 1842 he spent £215 on a beautifully ornate, eight-seater coach from the leading coachbuilder in Hastings, Rock & Baxter of 6 Stratford Place, White Rock. With coachman Stephen Elliott at the reins, four horses drew the magnificent vehicle. Mary Howitt remarked:

> Every year their father takes them a journey. He has a large carriage built like an omnibus, in which they and their servants can travel and in it, with four horses, they make long journeys. This year they were in Ireland, and next year I expect they will go into Italy. Their father dotes on them. They take with them books and sketching materials; and they have every advantage which can be obtained them, whether at home or abroad. Such were and are our friends the Leigh Smiths, and thou canst imagine how much pleasure we were likely to derive from such a family.'[4]

As each of his children reached 21, Smith broke with tradition by treating his daughters and sons alike, giving them investments which brought each an annual income of £300. He also gave Barbara the deeds of the Westminster school. The income placed Barbara in an extraordinary position for a woman in 1848. Whereas most women had little choice but to marry, bear children and live in subordination to their husbands, Barbara was free to live her life almost as she pleased. Money could not buy everything, however; for example her brother Ben went to Cambridge, but Barbara could not, since no university would admit women. In 1849 she attended Bedford Square Ladies College, where she studied art and politics.

At Pelham Crescent, Smith employed three live-in servants: Eleanor Nightingale was Barbara's lady's maid, Sarah Wise was parlourmaid, and John Gallop was their coachman. During her seventeen years there Barbara became acquainted with many notable people. In 1846 she met Bessie Rayner Parkes, whose parents were Mr Smith's tenants at 6 Pelham Crescent. Bessie wrote: 'until July, 1850, we were almost as one family, sheltered under the magnificent rock of the Castle Hill'. Other friends included Mary Howitt[5] and her children, Eliza Fox Bridell, Gertrude Jekyll, Marianne North and her father Frederick, one of the two Hastings' MPs, Miss Bayley of 2 Holloway Place and Ann Samworth[6] and her children, of Brooklands Cottage, a 'picturesque retreat' on Old London Road. The three Samworth girls and the three Leigh Smith girls enjoyed painting expeditions around Hastings. Through the Howitts she met Elizabeth Barrett Browning, Anna Jameson, Adelaide Procter and William Johnson Fox, the Unitarian minister.

Barbara took her painting seriously at a time when art was considered merely an ornamental accomplishment for ladies. In Hastings she met the painter William Holman Hunt, who lived during the winter in a house at the foot of the East Cliff. Barbara's tutor, W. Collingwood Smith, took her to meet John Hornby Maw in West Hill House. Through Miss Bayley she met George Scharf, later director of the National Portrait Gallery. She enjoyed the company of fellow artists such as the Pre-Raphaelites D. G. Rossetti and Lizzie Siddal.[7]

One lifelong friend was William Ransom, a printer and stationer based at George Street. He gave Barbara the means to get her radical ideas into print by publishing her women's emancipation articles in his newspaper, the *Hastings & St Leonards News*. From June to August 1848 Barbara wrote, under the pen-name 'Esculapius', *An Appeal to the Inhabitants of Hastings, Conformity to Custom* and *The Education of Women*.

In 1850 Bessie introduced Barbara to her cousin, Dr. Elizabeth Blackwell, the first woman physician; however, Barbara's cousin Florence Nightingale snubbed her Uncle Ben's illegitimate offspring. Barbara was introduced to Marian Evans in June 1852 but the two women did not become intimate friends until July 1856, when they shared a seaside holiday at Tenby in South Wales. Barbara was among the first to guess the true identity of the author of *Adam Bede* which Marian published under the pseudonym George Eliot in 1859. In the early 1860s they were neighbours, living only a few doors apart in Blandford Square. Barbara was the model for *Romola*, the eponymous heroine of a later novel.

As young women of 21 and 23, Bessie and Barbara were, extraordinarily, allowed to go unchaperoned on a walking tour of Belgium, Switzerland, Austria and Germany, visiting the painter Anna Mary Howitt in Munich. They discussed women's inferior status and how to change it. Barbara was well-informed, having studied political economy and law at Bedford Square Ladies College. She knew men would solidly resist sharing political power with women; they would fight to preserve their system, which served their interests perfectly. So, for the time being, the two indulged in a little personal liberation. Breaking with the orthodoxy of the day, they abandoned many trappings of femininity and ladylike behaviour and contrived a rather outrageous (but very practical) fashion of their own. They swanned about in heavy boots and wore blue tinted spectacles. For ease and comfort of walking they even cast off their corsets and shortened their skirts,[8] prompting Barbara to pen the lines:

> Oh! Isn't it jolly
> To cast away folly
> And cut all one's clothes a peg shorter
> (A good many pegs)
> And rejoice in one's legs
> Like a free-minded Albion's daughter.

In 1852, after a thorough study of primary education in London, Barbara opened Portman Hall School in Paddington, a non-denominational, unconventional school of mixed social class, which she ran for ten years with her friend Elizabeth Whitehead.

By 1853, Willie Leigh Smith was estates manager at Glottenham and Ben was studying for the Bar, so Smith gave up 9 Pelham Crescent and he and Barbara moved their base to London. Barbara frequently visited Hastings; the opening of the railway to London in 1851 shortened the journey from eight to just 2½ hours.[9] She stayed in lodgings or at 9 Pelham Crescent, where her sister rented rooms. Barbara lodged at Mrs. Samworth's in 1855 and painted her corn field, near the spot where Holman Hunt, had painted *Our English Coasts* three years earlier.

Tall and well-built, Barbara had a charisma and vivacity that seem to have captivated everyone. Dale Spender remarks that she is 'almost invariably portrayed... as a woman of glowing strength, active intelligence, warmth, understanding, and energy'.[10] Bessie Parkes described her as 'the most powerful woman I have ever known', and Matilda Betham Edwards said 'if the rare lot of supernumerary gifts ever fell to any one woman, that one was Barbara Bodichon'.[11] Jessie Boucherett described her as 'beautifully dressed, of radiant beauty, and with masses of golden hair' and historian Ray Strachey remarked:

> There seems to have been something particularly vigorous about Barbara Leigh Smith...Tall, handsome, generous and quite unselfconscious, she swept along, distracted only by the too great abundance of her interests and talents, and the too great outflowing of her sympathies... Life was a stirring affair for Barbara. Everything was before her - Art (for her painting was taken seriously by many eminent painters), philanthropy, education, politics - everything lay at her feet. The only trouble was to pick and choose.[12]

Crayon drawing of Barbara by Samuel Lawrence, 1880.

Indeed, Barbara had such a wide range of interests it is hard to see where she found the time for them. Among her pursuits was spiritualism: in 1853 she attended a series of séances in London with Rossetti, Bessie, and the Howitts. Matilda Betham Edwards said that Barbara was 'always endeavouring to crowd the activities and achievements of a dozen lives into one'[13] and 'always trying to make twelve hours do the duty of twenty-four, always taking her mental and physical powers to the straining point'.[14]

Barbara's zest for life, for doing not planning, and for seizing the moment, is clearly expressed in this letter to her friend Bessie Rayner Parkes:

Dearest Bessie

I have a great deal to say to you about *work*, & *life* & the necessity of *yr.* fixing early on a train of action, you I mean, what is so sad so utterly black as a wasted life, & how common! - I believe there are thousands of tens of thousands who like you & I *intend doing*, - *intend working*, but live & die, only intending.

I know something lovely about two girls under 20 both, who being left with little money and no near relations, left England and established themselves in Edinbro and kept a school in the worst part, and fed and still feed a light and a strong light in a place of utter moral darkness, they do it still and are both very *lively & happy* & are *perfectly independent* travelling when necessary by themselves and all that, they devote all their time to this object are quite rewarded by the good which is visible that they do, to their own eyes and everyone's, is not this very beautiful! ...

To be happy is to work, work, - work - for ever. But the soul must have some leisure, & that should be the communing with great souls, souls which can strengthen one another.

Barbara was deeply and passionately involved with four major campaigns: for married women's property rights, career opportunities, the vote, and higher education. In 1854 she wrote her first nationwide publication, *A Brief Summary, in Plain Language, of the Most Important Laws concerning Women*. Logical, patient and organised, she knew that the sensible way to begin a campaign was to define clearly the nature of the problem. She proved herself an excellent researcher and editor by sifting through all the complicated laws of Britain to extract and publish, in simple terminology, the legal disabilities and restrictions under which women lived. The pamphlet was later described as 'thin and insignificant looking, but destined to be the small end of the wedge which was to change the whole fabric of the law'.[15] It was widely read and discussed, and feminists Florence and Rosamund Davenport Hill, passed it to their solicitor brother Alfred, who took it to the Law Amendment Society, which appointed a committee to investigate the laws listed. When a woman married, everything she owned,

inherited or earned passed to her husband. Even if he deserted her, he kept her property.[16] This arrangement was so entrenched, and seemed so natural, that merely to criticise it was a radical act. Barbara assembled a small group, including Anna Jameson, Adelaide Ann Procter, Bessie Rayner Parkes and Mary Howitt and drafted a petition for women to retain their property on marriage. Seventy copies were made and distributed to like-minded women all over the country. This was Britain's first organised feminist action. The petition concluded that:

> it is time that legal protection be thrown over the produce of [women's] labour, and that in entering the state of marriage, they no longer pass from freedom into the condition of a slave, all whose earnings belong to his master and not to himself.

The idea was ridiculed in the press and criticised and mocked in drawing rooms nation-wide. The main objection was that it would disturb the 'natural' power of men over women. The counter-argument was that if such power is 'natural' it does not need man-made laws. The text of the petition was published in the *Hastings & St Leonards News.*[17] Editor William Ransom told readers they would find a copy of it at Mr. Winter's shop, 59 George Street.[18] Ransom had 'no doubt that many ladies will find their way thither to attach their names'.

Barbara's little circle grew and became known as the Langham Place group. In just one year the petition raised 26,000 signatures. The 70 parts were pasted together and presented in March 1856 to support the Married Women's Property Bill. Although it passed its first and second readings, the Lords blocked it.

Readers are invited to ponder for a moment how laborious and troublesome it was to disseminate ideas and distribute information in the 19th century. Imagine trying to run a campaign without computers, fax, email, photocopiers, radio or television. In the 1850s, there were not even telephones, cars or typewriters. Even the railways and the postal service were in their infancy. Barbara worked so hard that stress and over-exhaustion led to a serious nervous collapse in 1856.

Prior to this she had ended a love affair with her publisher John Chapman, who was married and was, by all accounts, a philanderer and a rogue. On a family trip to Algeria, Barbara met Frenchman Eugène Bodichon, a left-wing physician and anthropologist as unconventional as herself. She married him on 2 July 1857. 'Respectable' women did not have careers, so her decision to include her occupation - 'artist' - on her marriage certificate indicates disdain for convention and pride in being a professional woman. She also insisted on being called Barbara Leigh Smith Bodichon. For much of their marriage she spent six months a year with Eugène in Algeria and six in England, where she continued her feminist campaigning. During their seven-month honeymoon they travelled across the Atlantic third class and Barbara wrote *An American Diary.* They visited Dr. Elizabeth Blackwell, whom Barbara entreated to return to England.

Although the Married Women's Property Bill had failed, the

position of women was improved by the Divorce and Matrimonial Causes Act 1857, which revoked a husband's right to the earnings of a wife he had deserted, and which returned to divorced or legally separated women the property rights of a spinster. Just before she married, Barbara published a radical feminist booklet called *Women and Work* in which she asserted: 'No human being has the right to be idle ... Women must ... be trained to do some work in the world.' She called for equality of education and work opportunities and advocated employment for married women, citing nature as a precedent: 'Birds, both cock and hen, help one another to build their nest'. Again, this was an outrageous demand, and thought by some to be subversive. Barbara did not hold back; she argued that letting men hold all the financial resources and then refusing to admit women to any decently-paid work forced them to marry for financial support, which amounted to legal prostitution. Most of the 43 percent of women with no man to support them lived in poverty, which led many to succumb to casual prostitution. Barbara made plain that she meant interesting occupations not menial or domestic chores. She emphasised that women needed: 'WORK - not drudgery, but WORK'. Barbara later co-founded an employment bureau for women and the Association for Promoting the Employment of Women.

To appreciate just how remarkable Barbara was, one must keep in mind the context in which she operated. She criticised and challenged many of the most traditional and entrenched beliefs of the mid-1800s. Her ideas attacked almost everything the early Victorians held dear, the very fabric of English society: male chauvinism, racism and the class system. She once told a friend that while in Algeria 'Whenever rich people dined with me, I gave them just anything. When poorly-paid French functionaries were invited, I always provided a sumptuous repast'.[19] These were genuinely believed to be the Law of Nature and the Law of God - challenging either was blasphemous, even seditious. Barbara's bravery is breathtaking: in many cases hers was a solitary voice. But Barbara was a visionary; her ideals, then thought ridiculous and extreme, are now part of modern-day society. She lambasted the traits defined as correct 'feminine' behaviour: 'To think a woman is more feminine because she is frivolous, ignorant, weak and sickly is absurd.'[20]

She scrutinised the role of the consumer in perpetuating slavery, and advocated boycotting goods manufactured by exploitation: 'We can't expect the slave owner to give up his slaves when we rush with our money to buy the produce of this stolen labour'[21] and urged people to 'apply their conscience' when shopping. With Eugène, Barbara did much to improve hygienic conditions in Algeria by planting vast plantations of the American eucalyptus plant. In later life she used her own house as a night-school for undereducated and underprivileged working youths, farm labourers in particular. Her friend William Ransom at one time ran the school. In a letter to an aunt, Barbara wrote:

> I am one of the cracked people of the world, and I like to herd with ... queer Americans, democrats, socialists, artists, poor devils or angels; and am never happy in an English genteel family life.[22]

But of all her interests and passions, improving the situation of women was always closest to her heart. In 1858 Barbara purchased The *Englishwoman's Journal* and was able to disseminate her ideas more widely. It was distributed nationally and informed women about the rights movement. According to Matilda Betham Edwards, Edwards, Barbara 'had one subject even nearer to her heart than even the educational, material, and social elevation of her sex. [She] entertained a passionate pity for her pariah sister'[23] – i.e., those driven to prostitution.

Concurrent with her political activities, Barbara gained some renown as a painter of landscapes in watercolour and often exhibited her work to the public. She held a one-woman show at Gambart's French Gallery in 1859[24] and another in 1861, featuring forty-three of her drawings, mostly of Algerian landscapes and flora. Some are held at Hastings Museum; others are at Girton College, Cambridge. Of them, the *Hastings & St Leonards Observer* wrote:

> The scenes of Algerian landscapes are such that only a born artist would dare to paint. The most vivid colours are dashed about in wonderful profusion, and such a critic as Ruskin has spoken in terms of high praise of her clever work.[25]

When their father died in 1860 Ben inherited the Glottenham estates, Willie inherited Crowham Manor and Barbara inherited 5 Blandford Square. She also gained a private income of £1,000 a year. In 1863 she leased three acres from Ben and built a cottage in a pinewood clearing in Harding's Wood. It was near Scaland's Farm but on the road, so she called it Scalands Gate. This small house was built to Barbara's own design and specification. The internal walls were covered from floor to ceiling with Barbara's own paintings, and Gertrude Jekyll created the garden and photographed it in 1880. Here, Barbara entertained the eminent literary, artistic and political figures of the day including Frederick North MP and his daughter Marianne, Dean and Lady Stanley, Herbert Gladstone (son of the Prime Minister), the Brownings, Gertrude Martineau, Lord and Lady Brassey, Henry Fawcett MP, George Eliot, John Ruskin, Rossetti, Siddal and Mary Howitt, who wrote:

> Barbara has built her cottage upon the plan of the old Sussex houses, in a style which must have prevailed at the time of the Conquest. It is very quaint, and very comfortable at the same time.[26]

In the mid-1860s Barbara was active in the Kensington Ladies' Debating Society, of which Sophia Jex-Blake was a member. She realised that politicians would continue to ignore women until they had the means to unseat them by voting them out. The subject of votes for women had raised its head occasionally: Anne Knight founded a Female Political Association in 1847 and petitioned parliament; and in 1851 Harriet Taylor Mill had written about it in the *Westminster Review*.[27] However, the organised movement for women's suffrage really began on 8th May 1866, when Barbara wrote to Helen Taylor, step-daughter of John Stuart Mill MP, that she was 'very anxious to have some conversation with you about the possibility of doing something towards getting women votes'. This led to a petition which attracted 1,499 signatures. Elizabeth Garrett[28] and Emily Davies took it to Westminster and, feeling self-conscious, they asked the apple-seller to hide the huge petition under her stall while they waited for Mill. She agreed, but bid the ladies unroll it a little so that she could append her own signature. Mill, a philosopher and feminist who later published *The Subjection of Women*, accepted the petition and presented it to the House of Commons to support an amendment to the Reform Act that would give women the vote. It was defeated by 196 votes to 73.

Barbara printed and distributed penny booklets. One was *Objections to the Enfranchisement of Women Considered* (1866) and, according to Matilda Betham Edwards, she also wrote the anonymously-published *Illustrations of the operations of our Laws as they affects the Property, Earnings and Maintenance of Married Women* (1867).[29] In her 1872 pamphlet *Reasons for and against the Enfranchisement of Women* she claimed women's right to vote 'simply on the general ground that under a representative government, any class which is not represented is likely to be neglected.' Her chosen style was to examine the arguments against women's suffrage and demolish them one by one:

> 'Women do not want votes.' ... There are many men who do not care to use their votes, and there is no law compelling them either to register themselves or to vote... Make registration possible, and we shall see how many care to avail themselves of the privilege.

> The argument that 'women are ignorant of politics' would have great force if it could be shown that the mass of the existing voters are thoroughly well informed on political subjects, or even much better informed than the persons to whom it is proposed to give votes.

The campaign Barbara had started in 1856 for wives to hold property culminated in 1870 when the Married Woman's Property Act was passed. This allowed women to keep up to £200 pounds of their earnings and to inherit personal property and small amounts of money; everything else, whether acquired before or after marriage, belonged to their husbands.

One of Barbara's finest achievements was founding Hitchin College with Emily Davies – Britain's first university for women. This was later moved to, and renamed, Girton and eventually became part of Cambridge University. In her will, Barbara left £10,000 to Girton, ensuring its survival. She specified that this money must come from her earnings as a painter. (Her inherited wealth returned to her family). Three years after founding the college, Barbara and Emily organised a public meeting on higher education for women at the Assembly Rooms in St Leonards in 1872. A 'crowded and fashionable audience' heard from Hastings' most prominent people – its two MPs, Thomas Brassey and Ughtred Kay-Shuttleworth. Also present was another leading proponent of female education, Mrs. Maria Grey, who wrote *The Education of Women* in 1871.

In between all this political activity Barbara managed to spend time with Eugène and also with writer Matilda Betham Edwards, with whom she travelled in France and French Africa.[30] Barbara and Eugène had no children. Indeed, Barbara once said 'childbearing is the battlefield of women'.[31] Eugène died in 1885 and Barbara later suffered a stroke at her cottage at Zennor, Cornwall, after which she was an invalid. She asked Mr. E. Taught of Castle Road, Hastings to undertake her funeral, choosing a quiet country churchyard for her interment.

Barbara died in 1891. The funeral procession route was lined with hundreds she had helped to educate at Scalands Night School. The *Hastings & St Leonards Observer* wrote:

> Those who were present will never forget the sight so long as they live... From the house to the grave side sad faces and tear-rimmed eyes filled the roads... [Inside the church were heard] sobs that would not be stifled... She gave with a free hand, and left before the recipient had time to thank her... She was a true Englishwoman, of noble character, strong in purpose, and quick to act on any sensible suggestion, if someone would be blessed by it.

Later the paper remarked that:

> The deceased lady was a militant Radical, but she lived only to do good. The poor of Scalands Gate have sustained the loss of a warm sympathiser ... she housed and educated her labourers and their families... Her whole life was wrapped up in trying to elevate the poor, and alleviate the sufferings of all that were downtrodden.

Barbara was buried at St Thomas à Becket Church, Brightling. Her epitaph is now almost indecipherable and her name is absent from the guidebook's list of the notable people buried there. Her brother Ben, however, is thought worthy of inclusion, as an Arctic explorer. There was not even a Blue Plaque on 9 Pelham Crescent until April 2000, following requests by myself and others to Hastings Borough Council. After her death Scalands Gate was occupied by the Leigh Smith family until 1953 when it was given up. It remained empty and was partially destroyed by fire in 1955. It was rebuilt on the same site and still stands, as Scaland's Folly.

There is a curious connection between Barbara and the first woman MP. Her brother, Ben Leigh Smith, was rescued in the arctic in 1882 by fellow explorer Henry Gore-Booth, who had a 14 year old daughter, Constance. Twenty six years later, under her married name Markiewicz, she became the first woman elected to Parliament.[32]

FURTHER READING

Hirsch, P., (1998) *Barbara Bodichon,* Chatto & Windus

Burton, H., (1949) *Barbara Bodichon.* John Murray, London.

Holcombe, L., (1983) *Wives & Property,* University of Toronto Press.

Lacey, C., (1987) *Barbara Leigh Smith Bodichon & The Langham Place Group.* Routledge & Kegan Paul.

Spender, D., (1983) *Feminist Theorists.* The Women's Press. pp90-124.

Rendall, J.,1989, *Friendship and politics: Barbara Leigh Smith Bodichon and Bessie Rayner Parkes,* in Susan Mendus & Jane Rendall (Eds) *Sexuality and Subordination: interdisciplinary studies of gender in the nineteenth century,* p. 163.

REFERENCES

[1] The 1851 Census erroneously gave her birthplace as Watlington, Essex.

[2] For example Florence Nightingale.

[3] *Cinque Ports Chronicle & East Sussex Observer,* September 1838.

[4] Letter to Bessie Rayner Parkes, quoted by Madame Belloc, *In a Walled Garden,* 1895

[5] Mary Howitt, 1799-1888, Poet.

[6] Mrs Samworth died in 1883; her daughter Janet took over the house.

[7] Barbara arranged convalescent accommodation for Lizzie Siddal at 5 High Street in 1854.

[8] Compare this with Marianne North's similar sartorial alterations.

[9] Prior to this, the route was either by road and rail via Staplehurst Station, or by road throughout.

[10] Spender, D., (1990) *Women of Ideas.*

[11] Betham Edwards, M. (1919) *Mid Victorian Memories.*p.63

[12] Strachey, R., *The Cause,* 1928.

[13] Betham Edwards, M. (1919) *Mid Victorian Memories.* p.64

[14] ibid. p.78

[15] *The Englishwoman's Review,* 1891, p149.

[16] This system was called 'coverture'. Sir William Blackstone's *Commentaries on the Laws of England* (1765-69), decreed that 'the very being or legal existence of the woman is suspended during her marriage.' See Volume 1

[17] *Hastings and St Leonards News* 15th February 1856

[18] Later to be the home of Edith Chubb.

[19] Betham Edwards, M. (1919) *Mid Victorian Memories.* p.71

[20] *Women and Work,* 1857

[21] *Englishwoman's Journal,* 1863.

[22] Burton, 1949, p.92. Compare Barbara's comment with Marianne North's avoidance of gentility abroad.

[23] ibid

[24] A review of the exhibition appears in *The Illustrated London News,* 30 July 1859.

[25] December 10, 1891

[26] From Madame Belloc, *In A Walled Garden,* 1895.

[27] The editor was her husband, John Stuart Mill.

[28] Later Dr. Elizabeth Garrett Anderson, M.D.

[29] I personally do not think this a publication of Barbara's as there seems no reason for her to have published anonymously and this book was published in Edinburgh, while Barbara had no Scottish connections.

[30] See p 62.

[31] Betham Edwards, M. (1919) *Mid Victorian Memories.*p.74

[32] Though, as a Sinn Feiner, she never took her seat.

BESSIE RAYNER PARKES
Poet & Feminist
1829-1925

essie (Elizabeth) Rayner Parkes was the granddaughter of Joseph Priestley, a scientist and political reformer. She was born at Warwick and her Unitarian father had radical political views. Bessie took up photography briefly in her youth, then dropped it to concentrate on poetry and songwriting. Among her published work was *Poems* (1852) dedicated to Barbara Leigh Smith. *Hastings in Spring* includes the verse:

> Round go the windmill-sails, and children swarm
> At various games; the sick come slowly walking,
> Releas'd by this spring day, and you and I
> Will pace the High Street for an hour's grave talking--
> I mean that rais'd and sunny pavement, high
> Above the road, and bounded by a wall
> Which dear green trees o'erhang, quite undisturb'd,
> Save where our meditative shadows fall,--

In 1846, when Bessie was 17, her father leased 6 Pelham Crescent from Barbara Leigh Smith's father.

> A great domestic affliction caused us to take up our residence in Hastings--where, indeed, we were Mr. Smith's tenants--and until July, 1850, we were almost as one family, sheltered under the magnificent rock of the Castle Hill. Hastings was not then what it is now; the old town was widely separated from St. Leonards, and the lanes leading up to Ore Church were lanes of deep country seclusion.

Each family also had a house in Blandford Square, London. Bessie and Barbara were close friends and allies for twenty years, indeed almost inseparable for the first five. Bessie shared Barbara's commitment to legal reform for women, and in 1856 she published *Remarks on the Education of Girls*. Together they took over the editorship of the *Waverley Journal*, in 1856, and then co-founded the *English Woman's Journal*, with Bessie as editor. The *Journal* was the first feminist magazine, and it was printed by the Victoria Press, which employed only female compositors. The *Journal* was also a focal point for the Langham Place group. By November 1859, the journal had a regular circulation of 700 copies.

In 1866 Bessie published *Essays on Women 's Work,* which argued for improvements in girls' education. That same year, with Barbara, Bessie co-founded the first Women's Suffrage Committee.

Bessie also wrote and published several volumes of poetry.

Her conversion to Roman Catholicism in 1864 reflected her interest in the work of Sisters of Charity as a model for women's action. On a visit to France in 1867, Bessie met Louis Belloc. After a short courtship the pair married and Bessie abandoned her women's rights activities. She was never again active in, though was often sympathetic to, later feminist campaigns.

Bessie had two children. Her daughter, the novelist Marie Belloc-Lowndes, was a member of the women's suffrage movement. Her son, Hilaire Belloc, was a leading anti-feminist who opposed both votes and higher education for women. In 1910, Belloc, then an MP, proposed that votes for women should be given only to wives and mothers, as single women had failed to fulfil their responsibilities to society (i.e. to men). This was a display of sheer ingratitude to his sister, who had paid for his university education, without which he would have stood little or no chance of becoming an MP.

WOMEN & THE BRITISH MEDICAL PROFESSION
1849-1894

The process was so complicated that Lesley Hall produced this timeline.

1849 Elizabeth Blackwell obtains US M.D. degree in New York, U.S.A.
1859 General Medical Council admits her to UK Medical Register.
1860 New charter empowers GMC to exclude holders of foreign qualifications.
1862 Female Medical Society set up.
1864 Female Medical College opens: University of Zurich admits women students.
1865 Elizabeth Garrett obtains Licentiate in Medicine and Surgery of the Society of Apothecaries (which promptly closes the loophole allowing her to do so).
1866 Garrett opens Marylebone Dispensary.
1867 University of Paris admits women: Berne and Geneva follow suit.
1869 Sophia Jex Blake gains entrance to some Edinburgh courses.
1870 Garrett obtains Paris MD: becomes Medical Officer, East London Hospital.
1870 Edinburgh medical students riot against admission of women students.
1874 Founding of the London School of Medicine for Women.
1876 Russell Gurney's Enabling Act: Dublin College of Physicians licenses women.
1877 Royal Free Hospital admits women medical students for clinical training.
1878 University of London adopts new charter admitting women to degree courses.
1879 Sophia Jex-Blake attempts to set up college for medical women in Edinburgh.
1879 London School of Medicine for Women recognised for London medical degrees.
1880 20 women on Medical Register.
1885 the 3 Scottish medical corporations open to women.
1891 101 women doctors in practice.
1892 British Medical Association admits women doctors.
1894 Edinburgh University finally admits women medical students.

ELIZABETH BLACKWELL
Physician
1821-1910

Once described as a 'guiding star . . . to rebellious women everywhere,' Elizabeth was born in Counterslip, near Bristol, to a highly-cultured and prosperous family. They moved to the USA when she was 11 because her father had lost his business through fire and hoped to make good in the New World. The Blackwells lived in New York, Jersey City, and Cincinnati, and Elizabeth and her sisters received an excellent education from private tutors, comparable to that of their brothers. However, Mr. Blackwell died, leaving the family in poverty. Elizabeth, her mother and her two sisters opened a school at which they all taught in order to support themselves, and later Elizabeth taught in another school. In 1845 she decided to study medicine although it was considered ridiculous, unfeminine and even dangerous for women to do so. She studied privately during a period in which sixteen medical schools denied her admission. She was eventually admitted to Geneva College in New York, where she met with hostility on campus. She was barred from classroom demonstrations, and the towns-people and her fellow students ostracised and harassed her. However, on 23 January 1849 Elizabeth Blackwell became the first qualified female doctor in the modern world, ranking first in her class in the finals.

Elizabeth then moved to Paris to study surgery, but the hospitals spurned her. Only a midwifery school would take her, and there she became infected with gonorrhoea in her eye, while treating a child. The eye was lost and her surgical career was ruined.

Returning to England in 1850 no doctor would admit a woman to his practice, nor would anyone let practice rooms to a female doctor, so Elizabeth used her own house. She opened a one-room Dispensary for Poor Women and Children and, when her sister Emily[1] also graduated in medicine, they opened an Infirmary. In 1859 Elizabeth became the first woman listed on the British Medical Register. The following year, a new charter excluded holders of foreign qualifications.

Back in the USA the Blackwell sisters set up the Woman's Central Association of Relief, to train nurses for the Civil War, and a Women's

Dr. Elizabeth Blackwell in her parlour at Rock House, Exmouth Place.

Medical College, with Elizabeth as Professor of Hygiene. In 1869 Elizabeth moved permanently to England. She established a successful private practice and helped to organise the National Health Society in 1871. She became Professor of Gynaecology at the London School of Medicine for Women, founded by Elizabeth Garrett Anderson and Sophia Jex-Blake.

Other members of Elizabeth's family were women's rights pioneers. Her sister Antoinette was the first woman minister of religion and her brother married the American suffragist Lucy Stone, the first woman to publish a statement protesting about patriarchal marriage laws, and the first to retain her own name after marriage. Such was her fame that women who followed suit were known as 'Lucy Stoners.'

Elizabeth was a strong opponent of vivisection and vaccination and considered bacteriology to be nonsense. Her book *Counsel to Parents on the Moral Education of Children*, (1876) attracted controversy for dealing with sexual matters such as masturbation (of which she strongly disapproved). In 1879, Dr. Blackwell leased Rock House, a ten-room square house perched above the sea on the West Hill. Kitty, (Kathleen Barry, b. 1847) an Irish orphan whom she had unofficially adopted in 1853, moved with her, acting as her servant, secretary, housekeeper and companion.

In Hastings, Dr. Blackwell turned her attention to writing books, carrying out what was arguably her greatest work: reform. She wrote articles and letters to the local press about conservation, the environment and medicine, and took an active interest in local issues, opposing both the East Hill railway and the tramways. She attended public meetings about local issues; one was about alleviating poverty in Hastings. She stood for the Board of Guardians in 1885 but, to her relief, she was unsuccessful. In the late 1870s there was a proposal to amalgamate the Magdalen, Lasher and other charities to for a Hastings Grammar School Foundation to provide scholarships for boys, Dr. Blackwell opposed it, arguing for girls to be included. Her objection was ignored.

In 1883 she purchased Rock House and also bought two neighbouring, semi-detached houses in Dudley Road for her sisters Anna and Marian. Among the books Dr. Blackwell wrote at Rock House were:

The Human Element of Sex (1884)
Pioneer Work in Opening the Medical Profession to Women (1895)
Essays in Medical Sociology (1902)

Dr. Blackwell died at Rock House in 1910 and a memorial service was held on June 4th at St Clement's Church, though she was buried in Kilmun, Scotland, simply because it was a place she loved.

In June 1914, Hastings held a Pageant of Heroes. A huge procession of girls and women in their Sunday best greeted the national suffragist leader - Millicent Garrett Fawcett - at Hastings Station and proceeded to Exmouth Place, where more people had congregated, including a deputation of suffragettes. Mrs. Fawcett gave a speech and unveiled a memorial plaque.

Nearly forty years later, Dr. Effie Evers, wife of the Rector of Guestling, happened to upturn a white marble slab that lay in her pantry, which had been used for years for rolling out pastry. To her amazement she discovered it was a commemorative tablet inscribed to Elizabeth Blackwell, with just the barest amount of information and the Hastings Coat of Arms. The riddle of how and why it came to be there is, as yet, unsolved. Perhaps it was the original one, and the inscription was later considered to be inadequate. One story is that is was removed for safe keeping during the First World War. The Guestling Tablet was donated to the Royal Free Hospital in London in 1953 where it was set into the archway to the Dean's office.

The Pageant of Heroes in 1914: a procession to Rock House to unveil the memorial plaque to Elizabeth Blackwell.

REFERENCES

[1] In the USA Emily had found it almost impossible to get admitted to any medical school - even Geneva College barred women after Elizabeth had graduated.

SOPHIA JEX-BLAKE
Physician
1840-1912

Sophia Jex-Blake was born at 3 The Croft (now 16 Croft Road[1]), Hastings, in 1840 and was christened in St Clement's Church. She was educated at home until leaving for boarding school at the age of eight. Three years later she and her family moved to 13 Sussex Square, Brighton and, although she did not live in Hastings again, she did visit. For example, she appears in the 1871 Census, staying with her friend Ursula du Pré at 4, Parade.

As a child Sophia was 'stormy, tumultuous, and unmanageable'.[2] She excelled at maths but, when as a young woman she was invited to teach the subject at Queen's College, her father - a retired physician - refused to let her. He later relented, provided she declined a salary. While working in the USA Sophia met Dr. Lucy Sewell, and decided to become a doctor. She began to study, assisted by Dr. Elizabeth Blackwell. Before long, however, her father died and Sophia returned to England to look after her mother.

There was huge resistance from men against female doctors. Among the many objections was the notion that there was no call for them. Sophia responded to this in 1869 by writing,

> One argument usually advanced against the practice of medicine by women is that there is no demand for it; that women, as a rule, have little confidence in their own sex, and had rather be attended by a man... it is probably a fact, that until lately there has been "no demand" for women doctors, because it does not occur to most people to demand what does not exist; but that very many women have wished that they could be medically attended by those of their own sex I am very sure, and I know of more than one case where ladies have habitually gone through one confinement after another without proper attendance, because the idea of employing a man was so extremely repugnant to them.[3]

After a while she decided to try to get her medical training in England, but met with much obstruction from medical schools. She and four others managed to get admittance to Edinburgh in 1869 but they were repeatedly hindered by students, lecturers, professors and members of the General Medical Council. They tried to arrange women-only anatomy lessons but, as Sophia later wrote, 'certain all-powerful members of the Colleges of Physicians and Surgeons had resolved to ostracise any medical men who agreed to give us instructions.' Yet, when they tried to join the men's class, 'the same phalanx of opponents raised the cry of indelicacy'. In 1871 Sophia reported that

> ... the authorities had pledged themselves from the first to defeat our hopes of education ... Never have we applied for educational facilities of any kind but they have done their best to meet us with an uncompromising refusal, so far as it was in their power.
>
> The ill feeling culminated in an incident in which '...those [students] who had hitherto been quiet and courteous became impertinent and offensive; and at last came the day of that disgraceful riot, when the College gates were shut in our faces and our little band bespattered with mud from head to foot.

Owing to stress, Sophia failed her exams. She eventually took her degree at Berne University and, because of a new rule forbidding the holders of foreign degrees to practise in Britain, she was re-examined in Dublin and became the fifth woman on the British medical register. Sophia founded the London School of Medicine for Women and set up the first female practice in Edinburgh in 1878.

Sophia was an active member of the women's suffrage movement. She was a lesbian, and once said: 'I believe I love women too much ever to love a man.' [4] **In 1899 she retired to Windedene, Mark Cross, Sussex, with her long-term companion Dr. Margaret Todd. She died there, aged 72, and is buried at St Denys Church, Rotherfield.**

'Tis a beautiful thing, a woman's sphere!
She may nurse a sick bed through the small hours drear,
Brave ghastly infection untouched by fear,
But she mustn't receive a doctor's fee,
And she mustn't (oh shocking!) be called an MD,
For if woman were suffered to take a degree,
She'd be lifted quite out of her sphere![5]

[1] Unfortunately, the plaque on the house is today almost completely obscured by a hedge.
[2] Ray Strachey, 1928, *The Cause* (Bell & Son)
[3] Jex-Blake, S (1869) *Medicine as a Profession for Women.*
[4] Dr. Margaret Todd, 1918, *Life of Sophia Jex-Blake* p.65
[5] *The Englishwoman's Journal*, September 1875

EDITH CHUBB
Musician
1878-1975

dith Annie Chubb is believed to be the first woman in Britain to be awarded the B. Mus – the degree of Bachelor of Music. Born in Wellingborough, Edith was brought to Hastings when she was six. The family lived at 59 George Street, and was deeply involved in the church. The father, J. W. E. Chubb, was a licensed lay-preacher and organist at the Fisherman's Church.[1] Edith, too, was a lay reader and gave song recitals with organ accompaniment. Most unusually for girls, she and her sister were taught by their father to play the organ, along with their brother.

As a teenager Edith, trim and petite, with dark hair and blue eyes, improved her organ playing by studying under Mr. Baker Guy at St Clement's Church. Later, she was taught by the town's most eminent musician, Dr. John Abram, illustrious organist of St Paul's Church.[2] She also learned piano and was awarded the degree of Associate of the Royal College of Music and gained her B. Mus. at the age of just 19, as a non-collegiate student at the University of Durham. Her *Viva Voce* exam was conducted by Dr. Joseph Bridge, organist of Chester Cathedral.

Edith was an efficient and capable performer and, though not a virtuoso, she gave numerous organ recitals in Hastings and one at Harrogate. Her programmes contained difficult pieces including Basil Harwood's Dithyramb, Rheinberger's E-flat minor sonata and Sibelius' Finlandia.

Edith left Hastings to teach at St. Anne's School , Abbots Bromley, and at St. Katherine's Teacher Training College, London, where she was music instructor and chapel organist until her retirement. She was involved in various ways with professional bodies and became chairman of the Music Teachers' section of the Incorporated Society of Musicians, a position that brought her into contact with many prominent people. Edith learned to play 'cello and joined, with her sister, the Royal Choral Society, which gave all its concerts at the Albert Hall. They sang under many famous conductors including Sir Thomas Beecham, Gustav Holst, Sir Hugh Allen and Sir Malcolm Sargent.

When Edith retired in 1939, she returned to Hastings and bought Briarmead, 6 Fairlight Avenue, which she shared with her mother. During the Second World War, when the organist of St. Clement's Church joined the forces Edith took his position for the duration of the war. She founded the Old Town Choral Society, which gained a very high reputation. As a musician, she had a fine sense of judgement, quickly assessing the quality of music and performers. The Society gave several performances every year, usually at St. Clement's Church; at Christmas 1946 she conducted Handel's *Messiah* there, which was highly acclaimed by the Mayor. As her mother became increasingly infirm, Edith's activities were reduced. When her mother died, Edith was 71 and unable to realise her life-long ambition to travel. During the 1950s she was a councillor and treasurer of St Clement's Church and was instrumental in the church's acquisition of a new organ.

Edith did not hesitate to broadcast her strong views. Unhappy with the Hammond organ installed at the White Rock Pavilion she dashed off a critical letter to the local press. Edith had a keen sense of moral propriety and would attack issues that she felt were wrong. This usually involved letter-writing, sometimes to the newspapers. One victim was André Previn, conductor of the London Symphony Orchestra, whose extra-marital activities drew a letter of rebuke.

In her 90s, Edith moved to a nursing home in Ashburnham Road. She insisted on having an upper room, so she would get exercise from using the stairs. She died at the home in 1975, aged 97.

In 1999 Edith's association with Hastings Old Town was commemorated on her birthday, 10th October, when organist Julian Rhodes publicly dedicated a piece in his programme to her memory during a recital at All Saints' Church for Old Town Week. The piece was a Victorian march that was very popular in Edith's day.

ETHEL CHUBB

Edith's younger sister Ethel (1883-1924) was also well-known in Hastings. She was involved in St Clement's Church Sunday School; she founded St. Mary's Guild, and she was organist for the children's and Guild's Services. She taught First Aid, French, and lacemaking. She wrote and staged a play called *The Other Wise Men* and gave interesting lectures on various topics. She was organist at St George's, Brede, during the First World War, where she wrote a new voluntary each week and trained a good choir. The long journey, and the cold church, were said to have contributed to Ethel's untimely death from tuberculosis at the age of 41.

---

[1] He was also an outspoken, right-wing reactionary. See Mike Matthews, 1991, *Alf Cobb: Mugsborough Rebel.* A photograph of Mr. Chubb is displayed in the Fisherman's Museum.

[2] St Paul's Church was a magnificent edifice on the corner of Church Road and Ellenslea Road, St Leonards. Unfortunately, it was demolished in the 1960s.

Lady Annie Brassey, the first woman to circumnavigate the globe.
Photograph taken on board the yacht *The Sunbeam*, pictured below.

LADY BRASSEY
Traveller, collector & writer
1839-1887

Lady Brassey, née Anna Allnutt, was the first woman to circumnavigate the globe. She grew up in an art-collecting family and at the age of 21 married a railway millionaire's son, Thomas Brassey. The Brasseys built a magnificent country mansion, Normanhurst Court, at Catsfield, just outside Hastings and also maintained a London home at 24 Park Lane, later the Lady Brassey Museum and now the site of the Hilton Hotel. Their third home, built in Venetian Gothic style, is now Hastings Library.

The couple had a son and three daughters, one of whom died aged five. In 1868 Thomas was elected Liberal MP for Hastings; he was knighted in 1881 and raised to the Peerage in 1886.

While Tom was a sailing enthusiast, Annie had never been to sea, but she quickly found her 'sea legs' and enjoyed trips on Tom's two yachts. After Tom qualified as a Master Mariner in 1873 he commissioned *The The Sunbeam*, a 'sail-and-steam' schooner measuring 190' x 38'4, equipped with three-masts and a 64hp, 2-cylinder steam engine. Its opulence was unsurpassed. A guest wrote:

> The Sunbeam is quite a floating palace fitted up in the most luxurious manner. Her many saloons and sleeping cabins are marvels of elegance and comfort, while the taste of Lady Brassey is displayed in the numberless pictures and curios which adorn the walls and tables in the different apartments.

On 6 July 1876 *The Sunbeam* left Cowes with eleven 'non-crew persons' on board (Annie included the Commander, the Captain and the Surgeon in this list) and a crew of 32 (including the Nurse, Lady's Maid and Stewardess). The couple's four children and the family pets went along, and many guests embarked and disembarked at various points, which included Madeira, Tenerife, Cape de Verde Islands, Palma, Rio de Janeiro, the River Plate, the Straits of Magellan, Chile, Santiago, Valparaiso, Tahiti, the South Sea Islands, the Sandwich Islands, Honolulu, Japan, Canton, the Pearl River, Macao, Singapore, Ceylon, and the Suez Canal. *The Sunbeam*

MRS. BRASSEY AT HOME at NORMANHURST

"WOMAN'S SPHERE"
(*Hastings & St Leonards Observer*, 22 May 1880, *from the Whitehall Review.*)

Slightly bronzed I find her, with spray of many seas and suns of many climes, but the blue stocking is from first to last conspicuous by its absence. No woman's rights, no prate of Girton College are dinned into my ears. We talk chiefly of women, it is true, but of woman as we chiefly find her, domesticated in her home duties and fulfilling them, not coveting the burdens of the stronger sex. ...

"It is chiefly domestic business that I get through here. My original matter is usually composed aboard the Sunbeam, but I revise it for the press when I reach home ... I am awake at six, sometimes earlier, even at four. Then I write as I lie in bed; my writing materials are already by my side. At seven o'clock the post comes, at 8.30 I see my secretary in here, and we go through the sketch of morning correspondence. By then my letters for immediate post are written, or proofs corrected, if any are waiting. Then come the stud groom for orders, and the head servants of each department for their daily instructions"...

"Do you advocate what is called 'higher education' for women?"

"I think that girls should, prima facie, be educated for that which I consider women to be designed for – to be an helpmate for man... I think the more a girl can accept education all round the better fitted she will be to play the part of wife ... Girls should acquire a stock of information by sound but not too dry reading. Without being blue, they may with advantage be able to talk to a ball-room or dinner-table companion on something less frivolous than the room decorations or their neighbour's dress."

"Then you don't approve of scientific education for girls?"

"... her requirement in life is to be educated to assist man hereafter. As a rule, time is too short to enable her to qualify both scientifically and socially..."

"Do you approve of women taking a political line? I do not mean in agitations but through the mediums of Society - organisation of political drawing rooms?"

"I think such réunions of immense advantage to political parties, but to do it well a woman must have a specialité for it, and she can have no time in that case for thorough attention to children, household, literature, or out-door pursuits, or general aid to her husband." ...

[During his ride to Battle station the reporter concludes:]

"not till now had I fully realised that never is woman so womanly as when claiming her primary and Biblical right to fulfil her main mission in creation – that of an helpmate to man".

arrived back at Hastings Pier at 01:45am on 26th May 1877. While Annie attended the morning service at St Paul's Church, workmen unloaded 140 packages of curiosities, including an elk, various dogs, monkeys, some rare, exotic plants and 20 cages of birds. The voyage of *The Sunbeam* and the prestige of Thomas Brassey, who became Civil Lord of the Admiralty in 1880, made the yacht-master's certificate fashionable in a limited circle of wealthy men.

As the Brasseys were Hastings' greatest celebrities, local civic dignitaries were anxious to welcome them home with as much pomp and circumstance as they could. After weeks of planning by a special committee, a magnificent banquet was held at the Pier Pavilion, at which 300 paying guests enjoyed 28 courses (provided by the *Queen's Hotel*), while singers and musicians entertained them. A ballad entitled *Sunbeams* was performed. This was written for the occasion by W. Glenister of Queen's Road, and was dedicated to Annie.

The brilliantly-lit pier was adorned with bunting and crowded with people. However, the high price of admission prevented the attendance of anyone from the lower classes. This point was raised in the local paper: the editor was incensed that the working classes had been excluded from welcoming the Brasseys when their affection for the couple was equal to that of the wealthy, invited guests.[1]

Thomas Brassey was repeatedly extolled in a series of overweening speeches and toasts. In his reply, he stated that 'any merit ought to be shared very largely with my dear wife'. This received rapturous applause. He went on to reveal that, because of various difficulties, at one point he had seriously contemplated splitting the voyage into two. He consulted his wife, who urged him to continue. He declared that it was thanks to 'the wisdom of her counsel' that the *The Sunbeam* became the first yacht to circumnavigate the globe. Annie later gave a very short speech of thanks to the organisers and well-wishers.

Annie's journal of all the difficulties and pleasures of the trip was published in 1878 as *A voyage in the Sunbeam: our home on the ocean for eleven months*. It described a seagoing version of their luxurious, upper-class Victorian lifestyle, centred on the drawing room and children's nursery. It was her third book, and Annie was surprised when it became an overnight best-seller. It later went to nine editions and was translated into 17 languages. This extract from her final book describes the fun and the wonderful sights, as well as her indisposition:

Left Excerpts from an interview with Lady Brassey at her country house, Normanhurst, by a reporter from the *Whitehall Review*, reprinted in the *Hastings & St Leonards Observer*, 22 May 1880. It is rather incongruous that the reporter sneers at 'blue stockings' (i.e. educated women) and denounces talk of Girton College for Women as mere "prate", when just four years earlier, Lady Brassey's husband had donated to Girton the modern day equivalent of a quarter of a million pounds. He later became a prominent advocate of votes for women. Ironically, it appears that Mr. Brassey was more of a feminist than was his wife.

Thursday May 19th. - Wind fair, but head-swell still continuing. I had a very busy morning below, writing journal and letters. At noon we had run 120 miles under sail, and were then in lat. 36° 12' S., long. 122° 4' E. In the afternoon we took some photographs of Tom in his R.N.A.V. uniform, the Guard of Honour, ourselves, the Court, &c., on the occasion of Neptune's visit when we crossed the line. Sundry unsuccessful attempts were made to photograph the animals, but they seemed to be suffering from a severe attack of the fidgets. To see 'Jenny Jenkins,' the monkey, in her new blue jumper with 'Sunbeam R.Y.S.,' embroidered by Mabelle, and 'Mr. Short,' the black-and-tan terrier, playing together, is really very pretty; they are so quick and agile in their movements that it is almost impossible to catch them. 'Mrs. Sharp,' the white toy terrier, in her new jersey, a confection of Muriel's, occasionally joins in the frolic; though her condescension is not much appreciated, for she is rather too quick with her teeth. The photograph of the Guard of Honour was spoiled by a passing whale, to which Tom suddenly drew everybody's attention by pointing to it with his drawn sword. The monster left a greasy wake behind him, as he swam lazily along, blowing slightly.

Towards evening the air became very cold, and the wind not quite so fair. A splendid sunset threw a lovely glow on the sails. Later on the sea continued to go down, and I was able to make my first appearance at dinner at sea for many a long day past, but only as a spectator even now.[2]

Annie amassed an enormous number of artefacts from many different cultures and countries. (Two black pug-dogs, purchased in China, are the ancestors of all the black pugs in Britain.) She wanted everyone to see the treasures, not to hide them away or sell them to upper-class people. As Julian Porter[3] notes, Annie 'was more like a museum curator than a collector.' *The Sunbeam* was often moored off Hastings, and people were ferried across at a shilling a head to see Annie's collections.

The collections have since been scattered. Her photographs reside in the Huntington Library, California, but many items are in the museums at Bexhill and Hastings. The Durbar Hall, in Hastings Museum, was originally constructed for the Indian & Colonial Exhibition of 1886. It was purchased by the Brasseys and reconstructed at their London home, to make the Lady Brassey Museum. In 1919, after Thomas's death, it was donated to Hastings Corporation and became an annexe to the Museum in 1932. The Lower Hall contains displays from the Indian sub-continent: jewellery and costumes, antiquities from Burma, and a tiger head. The Upper Hall focuses on the life of the Brasseys, and boasts a model of *The Sunbeam*, and exotic artefacts collected on various voyages.

The magnificence of her collection, her fascinating books and the extraordinary voyages she made have eclipsed somewhat Annie's other activities. She was a central figure in Hastings' upper-class social life, and

she performed much charity work. Her favourite good cause was the St John's Ambulance service and, in 1881, in recognition of her work in promoting it all over the world, she was honoured with an award of Dame Chevalière of St John of Jerusalem. Her daughter Idina carried on this work into the twentieth century. She was involved with local politics, and helped her husband to canvass the local electorate, but she does not seem to have been active in the feminist movement. Her husband however was a lifelong supporter of women's rights and in 1876 he donated £2,500 of the £6,000 needed to enlarge Girton College, the establishment founded by feminists, including Barbara Bodichon, to improve women's education.

During another long voyage, Annie died on *The Sunbeam* after contracting malaria, at the age of just 48. She was committed to the sea: a true sailor's burial, in the Indian Ocean between Australia and Mauritius. Thomas erected a beautiful memorial to her at Catsfield Church.

Thomas was knighted in 1881 and raised to the peerage in 1886. In 1890 he remarried, and with his wife Sybil de Vere Capel, became very a prominent campaigner for women's suffrage.

Further reading

Brassey, Annie, 1878, *A voyage in the Sunbeam. Our home on the ocean for eleven months*.

Brassey, Annie, 1880, *Sunshine and storm in the East. Or cruises to Cyprus and Constantinople*.

Brassey, Annie, 1885, *In the Trades, the Tropics and the Roaring Forties. 14,000 miles in the Sunbeam in 1883*.

Brassey, Annie,1889, *Three voyages in The Sunbeam*.

Brassey, Annie, 1889, *The Last voyage, to India and Australia, in The Sunbeam*.

Wright, B, 1885, *A Catalogue Raisonné of the Natural History, Ethnographical Specimens and Curiosities Collected by Lady Brassey during the Voyages of the 'The Sunbeam', 1876-1883*.

REFERENCES

1 *Hastings & St Leonards Chronicle*, 4 July 1877.

2 Brassey, Annie, 1889, *The Last voyage in the Sunbeam*. p.259

3 Librarian at Bexhill, in his Master's dissertation about Lady Brassey's collections.

Left Elsie Bowerman in 1928, aged 38. This photograph was published in the *Evening Standard*, to accompany her article *Why Women Do Not Write Utopias*.

Right Elsie at the age of 23, holding copies of *Votes for Women*. She is standing at the corner of Claremont and White Rock, Hastings. Suffragettes had to stand in the gutter to avoid being arrested for obstructing the pavement.

The photograph was published in the *Hastings & St Leonards Observer*, 24th April 1913. The caption read: 'During this week the local Suffragettes are holding a Self-Denial Week. In the above picture Miss Bowerman, who was one of the rescued passengers of the "Titanic", is seen soliciting subscriptions from passers-by.'

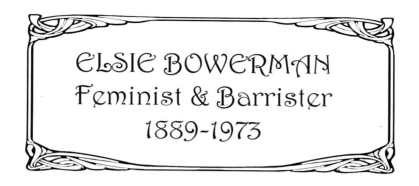

ELSIE BOWERMAN
Feminist & Barrister
1889-1973

Elsie Bowerman's mother, Edith Barber, lived at Sinnock Cottage, Hastings Old Town, and worked as a draper's assistant. About 1888 she married her employer, William Bowerman. He was a town councillor from 1885-88 and owned rental properties and a chain of drapers' shops in Hastings and St. Leonards, in which he employed ten people.[1] William was 58 and Edith 25 when Elsie was born, on 18th December 1889 at Tunbridge Wells. In 1890 William sold his chain of shops and retired. The 1891 Census indicates that he was 'living on own means' at 145 London Road, St Leonards, with his wife, baby daughter and two servants.

Elsie was raised in comfortable, but unostentatious circumstances. Her parents took great interest in public affairs, both local and national, and believed that happiness lay in working for others. Although wealthy, her parents were careful with money. William frequently appealed against local rates and had many rental properties reassessed in his favour, a practice continued by his wife and daughter after his death. His accumulation of properties is central to Elsie and Edith's future since it provided an unearned income without which their lives might have been very different. William died in 1895 and Edith erected choir-stalls in his memory in St. Matthew's Church, Silverhill. A commemorative brass plaque is attached, facing the organ.

One of Elsie's earliest memories was of Sunday evenings when her father played hymns on the piano.[2] She took private piano lessons from Fraulein Bischoff at Hastings & St Leonards Ladies College,[3] and in 1900 passed her examination with Honours. In 1901 Elsie was sent as a boarder to the prestigious Wycombe Abbey School. Then 11, she was the youngest girl there. Elsie recalled that 'the anticipated tears were firmly suppressed'. Such early independence and long separations from home stood her in good stead for her later travels. Her intelligence became evident when she achieved first place in a form of eleven girls nearly two years her senior.

Elsie left school in April 1907 and stayed a while in Paris before beginning her studies in Mediaeval and Modern Languages at Girton College, Cambridge. She was elected representative of first year

In 1907, Edith, now 43, married 67-year-old Alfred Chibnall, a wealthy farmer.[4] This union is somewhat mysterious: it appears that they split up within two years, certainly before 1910, from which time Edith began to use the name 'Mrs. Bowerman Chibnall' instead of 'Mrs. Chibnall'. He is omitted from Elsie's correspondence, is missing from her photograph collections and did not accompany Edith and Elsie on their holidays. When Alfred died in 1929 he left his entire estate of £10,000 to male friends. Perhaps he disapproved of his wife's involvement in politics.

By 1910 there were six societies in Hastings campaigning for women to have the parliamentary vote. Edith and Elsie joined the most militant: the WSPU, which had been founded in 1903 by Mrs. Pankhurst in Manchester and spread throughout Britain. Edith was in addition an official of the Women's Tax Resistance League and, during the university holidays, Elsie was an Organiser for the Hastings Branch of the WSPU.[5] At Girton, Elsie wore suffragette badges in lectures, shared and sold copies of *Votes for Women* and organised suffrage debates. Edith joined a deputation to Parliament in 1910, which the police obstructed and which turned violent, resulting in 119 arrests and many injuries. Using notepaper and envelopes with 'Votes for Women' blindstamped, Elsie wrote to Edith:

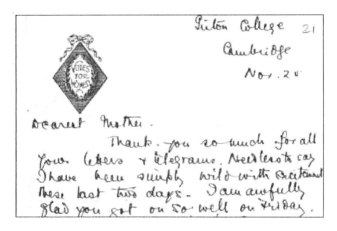

... Needless to say I have been simply wild with excitement these last two days... I am awfully glad you got on so well on Friday ... What a pity it seems that you have to go through it all again tomorrow... I shall be frightfully anxious to hear how you fare.

Edith was, in fact, injured on her second deputation.

Dearest Mother, Thank you for your letter received this morning. I am so sorry you have had such a bad time. It is sickening that this endless fighting has to go on. I am frightfully sorry Mrs. Pankhurst & Mrs. Haverfield were arrested.

In 1911 Elsie, aged 21, passed the Cambridge Tripos examination with a Class II degree and around this time she also came into her inheritance from her father. This included a number of rental properties to which she added by further purchases. The income they provided left Elsie free from the necessity to work. She and her mother had a large income: in 1918 Elsie's unearned income amounted to over £700 p.a., the equivalent of about £70,000 today. However, neither of them indulged in extravagant purchases or high living. They lived modestly, mending not replacing, buying sale goods, and saving money whenever they could. Their 'penny-wise' attitude is exemplified in a letter from Elsie in Paris, in which she warns her mother to bring her own soap as, to her annoyance, she was charged a franc by the hotel for one bar. Yet, just months later, they blew £55 on two first-class tickets to New York on board the most luxurious and glamorous steamship ever built.

In April 1912, Elsie and Edith, now aged 22 and 48, travelled from Warrior Square station to Southampton. They were to visit William Bowerman's relations, and a friend, Mr Guthrie, in Ohio, and would afterwards travel across the USA and Canada. They occupied Cabin 33 on Deck E of the *RMS Titanic*, which set off on 12th April. The story of its sinking, two days later, is so well-known it need not be repeated. Over 1000 were drowned, but the famous 'women and children first' tradition, supplemented by the less-often quoted 'first class passengers take priority' maxim ensured that Elsie and Edith were among the 700 saved. Elsie wrote:

> The silence when the engines stopped was followed by a steward knocking on our door and telling us to go on deck. This we did and were lowered into life-boats, where we were told to get away from the liner as soon as we could in case of suction. This we did, and to pull an oar in the midst of the Atlantic in April with ice-bergs floating about, is a strange experience.

The two women were in Lifeboat 6 with about 22 others including Frederick Fleet, the lookout who had first spotted the iceberg. The 1997 film *Titanic* featured several scenes in this lifeboat because it accommodated two of the main characters, Molly Brown and the fictional Ruth Dewit Bukater, mother of the heroine Rose. The boat was the third to be lowered, at 0055hrs. Lifeboat 6 was under the command of Quartermaster Robert Hitchens, who would later come under intense attack for not saving more passengers. Captain Smith, through a megaphone, ordered the lifeboats to come back to pick up more passengers, but they did not respond. Robert Hitchens refused to go back because he feared that, when the *Titanic* sank, she would produce a suction force and the boilers would explode, killing everyone on the lifeboats. One source claims that Molly demanded that the women be allowed to row to keep warm. Hitchens, protested, but Molly told him he would be thrown overboard if he attempted to stop her. Both men eventually gave in and Molly took control. She ordered the women to row and distributed her furs and other clothing to the freezing passengers.

The boat floated in the middle of the Atlantic all night before being rescued at 0600 and taken to New York by the Carpathia. They were reported safe by *Cleveland Plain Dealer* and the *Hastings & St Leonards Observer*. Undeterred, they continued with their itinerary, stayed at a ranch in British Columbia and visited the Klondyke and Alaska. During the trip Elsie wrote an article for the *Wycombe Abbey Gazette* entitled '*The Magnetic North'*. The pair returned to Hastings as minor celebrities: they were the only *Titanic* passengers from the town. Edith and Elsie resumed their suffrage activities, publicising meetings and selling ice-cream for the cause.

Their nightmare voyage to New York did not deter either from travelling: they visited Arundel and Loch Lomond in 1913, Betts-y-Coed, Winchester and Rome in 1914, and Dartmoor in 1915. Photographs taken in 1915 show Elsie and her mother in the garden at Heathfield, their country house in Thakeham, with a few close friends, such as the Hon. Evelina Haverfield, Mrs. Peirce, and Miss Hogg and Miss Tristram, both Hastings suffragettes. Few men appear; Mr. Guthrie was one. In contrast to many photographs of middle-class women of that era, Elsie and her young friends were not at all ladylike or dainty; they happily lolled about on the grass with their pets and Edith is seen gardening. Elsie was a sturdy woman of average build: 5' 5', with thick brown wavy hair with a centre parting, blue eyes, a low forehead, square chin, straight nose, round face, full mouth and fair complexion. She appears open and sincere, almost tomboyish, with a zest for life, and completely without airs, graces or coquetry.

In July 1916 the Honourable Mrs. Haverfield, now a leading light in the pro-war movement, invited Elsie to go to Serbia as a motor driver. Although 26 years old, Elsie begged her mother's permission:

> Mrs Haverfield has just asked me to go out to Serbia at the beginning of August, to drive a car - May I go? ... It is what I've been dying to do & drive a car ever since the war started. I should have to spend the week after the procession learning to drive - the cars are Fords ... It is really like a chance to go to the front. They want drivers so badly. So do say yes - It is too thrilling for words.

When Edith consented Elsie thanked her, adding, 'It is good of you always to be so splendidly unselfish - everyone I have met is fearfully envious of me having the chance to go.' However, a different job was found for Elsie: in September, she became an orderly in the London Unit of the now-famous Scottish Women's Hospitals, run by Dr. Elsie Inglis.[6]

The all-female unit had to travel by a most circuitous route - via Scandinavia, Archangel, Moscow and Odessa - to serve the Serbian and Russian armies in Romania. Unfortunately it arrived just as the allies had been defeated. English newspapers carried reports about the women's units, which, Elsie wrote, 'make us afraid you will all think we are starving or dead or something whereas we are really having the time of our lives.' In November 1916 they set up a hospital near the Danube, then had to dismantle it and join the retreat to the Russian frontier. It was bitterly cold and Elsie asked in her almost daily letters home for gloves, scarves and thick stockings, as well as a dozen Kodak Brownie films, Suchard chocolate, and a book of Robert Louis Stevenson's stories. However, she begged her mother not to send Christmas puddings. In addition to her many letters, Elsie sent telegrams at every opportunity. Despite this, Edith wrote several frantic letters to the headquarters of the Scottish Women's Hospitals from whom she received repeated reassurance that Elsie's unit was safe.

Elsie found the experience wonderful. In her detailed pencil-written diary she described pitching tents for the field hospital and serving meals to 250 people with the help of only one Russian, who could not speak English. She told of sleeping in the open just twenty miles from the firing line, of having singing parties with soldiers around camp fires and of cross-country rides with Russian officers. She was in charge of wagon-loads of equipment which frequently got lost and had to be recovered, and all this in the midst of a war. Although Elsie was an orderly, she sometimes helped with the wounded. However, on 1st March she wrote in her diary 'Life is one long chuckle at present' and described her shopping sprees, and commented that she sometimes deliberately left her purse behind to curb expenditure. She was in St Petersburg in 1917 and her diary contains not only eye-witness testimony of living in the midst of the Russian Revolution, but it reveals something of her personality, her use of language, and her interests and priorities.

March 13th, 1917.

Great excitement in street - armoured cars rushing up and down - soldiers and civilians marching up and down armed - attention suddenly focussed on our hotel & house next door - rain of shots directed on to both buildings as police supposed to be shooting from top storeys - most exciting. Several shots went through windows. Presently our hotel searched by rebels - came into each room searching for police spy - very nice to us - most polite - several civilians as well as soldiers. One 'revolutionary' came into our room to dress - didn't know how to wear his sword - we had to assist with the strapping up. Much to our disgust all hotel servants also the manager disappeared - nothing to eat - picnicked in our rooms. Shooting & shouting continuously all day in the street - several search parties through the hotel at intervals. V. difficult to settle down to anything - sat at hotel window in afternoon, watched crowds in streets, lorries crowded with armed men.

Youths left in charge of the hotel kitchen - armed with ferocious carving knives & muskets. Managed to loot some glasses of milk - all other food locked up. Fresh alarm in hotel in evening when rifle shot suddenly heard in the building. Merely one of the revolutionary sentries. Banged rifle on floor in his excitement & shot went through the ceiling. Rumour that hotel will be fired during the night so we packed our haversacks carefully in case we had to make hurried departure in the night. Retired to bed. Great luck to share such comfortable quarters. [Hotel] Astoria has been sacked & guests turned out. [Female colleagues] went to Embassy in afternoon in case there were any orders for British people - didn't get any enlightenment. They 'wished us luck' - no other suggestions to offer. At intervals during the day motors rush by - scattered news-sheets & declarations to the people. [Nurses] Brown & Hedges ran into street affray - had to take cover in a canal.

March 14th

Crowds in streets but much quieter than yesterday. Soldiers maintaining order. Passed houses which had been occupied by police etc where papers in piles burning in the streets - still being thrown on by soldiers. Headquarters of police & detective force burnt to the ground & still burning - people firing at a police stronghold in house above us ... rushed across to take refuge in a church doorway - found the shots were being sent in that direction - presently soldiers came rushing into the building with pistols so we decided to move into doorway of a house in the courtyard - but soldiers came pouring in so we decided to get out while we could. Got out before things became any warmer.

Throughout we have met with the utmost politeness & consideration from everyone. Revolutions carried out in such a peaceful manner really deserve to succeed. Today weapons only seem to be in the hands of responsible people - not as yesterday, carried in many cases by excited youths. Heard that the ministers have now surrendered. Some have been shot, or shot themselves.

March 15th

[Visited] Anglo-Russian hospital - thankful we are not staying there. They have been under orders to stay indoors all through the revolution - Hotel now quite organised again. Meals etc as usual. Reported that 3600 people have been killed & wounded in street affrays. People have decided to ask the Tsar to abdicate in favour of his son.

March 17th

In afternoon went down Nevski [Prospect]. Huge crowds in every direction. Presently motor came along - people flocked around - officer & also man in civilian dress made two announcements from the car - viz., that the Tsar had abdicated in favour of his brother Michael &

Michael had placed the power in the hands of the people, therefore to all intents & purposes Russia is now a republic. 2.30pm Mar 16th 1917. People cheered and cheered - wildest excitement. Rushed off & fetched ladders to take down the eagles off various public buildings. Rumour that there is a sanguinary revolution in Berlin & that the Kaiser is dead! Seems too good to be true. We spent the evening in wild speculation.

March 17th - 23rd

Went with Walker to be manicured - Went to Russian church in station square. Very full - so came away to another - also crowded. Railway through Finland reopened so we may possibly return home via Norway- We are told we shall have utmost discomfort - no accommodation food or water. Don't mind if we can only get off home - Eagles on Winter Palace all draped with Red.

March 24th - 25th

Got up 5 am. To station. People at that hour already standing in long queues outside bread shops. Train left 7.40. Very comfy. Travelled through Finland. Sat outside train on step for a long way. Delightful restaurant car and sleeping berths. [25th] Arrived at Tornea Finnish frontier 12 noon. Drove in sleigh over river to Customs House. On by sleigh to Haparanda in Sweden - Drive in sleigh over snow through woods. Most comfy sleighs could lie right back - 1st class sleeping berths most delightful train - spotlessly clean - nice women attendants.

After a short stay in Sweden the unit made its way back via Bergen and Aberdeen, to London Euston Station. Elsie made straight to Mrs. Peirce's house in Highgate, arriving at midnight on 4th April 1917.

On her return to England, Elsie divided her time between her country house at East Lavington and London, where she was a member of the University Club for Ladies. She received the Certificate of the Russian Medal for Meritorious Service. Never one to rest on her laurels, she soon became involved in another round of public work.

When the war broke out, the suffrage movement had placed its demands on the back-burner. The WSPU became The Women's Party and encouraged women to volunteer for war work and men to sign up; it opposed pacifism and socialism and tried to halt strikes. Elsie joined the Women's Party and soon became a paid Organiser. For several months she toured nation-wide with the famous WSPU leaders Flora Drummond and Emmeline and Christabel Pankhurst. At each town, Elsie took lodgings and set about organising and advertising mass-meetings: one at Manchester drew 10,000 people. Her sphere of responsibility eventually extended as far as Devon, where she was organising meetings right until the end of the war. She often shared the platform with Christabel Pankhurst.

> **MISS CHRISTABEL PANKHURST IN BATH**
> **PATRIOTIC WOMEN'S MEETING**
>
> Miss Christabel Pankhurst addressed a well-attended patriotic women's meeting at the Guildhall on Thursday, and his Worship the Mayor was in the chair. Upon the platform were the Archdeacon of Bath and Mrs. Fish, the Mayoress, Mrs. Maynard, and Miss Elsie Bowerman (Clifton), the District Organiser of the Women's Party.[7]

More than once while on tour Elsie was mistaken for one of the Pankhurst girls. Elsie found the events 'thrilling' and felt passionate about her endeavours. She wrote to Edith: 'It makes one so angry to think that people should need to be urged to patriotism at a time like this.'

In 1918 Elsie became one of the first women Election Agents when she acted in that capacity for Christabel Pankhurst, who stood unsuccessfully for the Women's Party at Smethwick, in the first General Election in which women were permitted to stand as candidates.[8]

Aspects of Elsie's personality are revealed in her letters to Edith during her nation-wide tour. Examples of her snobbery, intolerance, faultfinding and complaint include: 'how tired one gets of the Yorkshire accent - it IS hideous. I do hope I shan't catch it.' She sacked her letting agent, Chennells, of Hastings, and took personal control of the rent collection and maintenance of her properties, employing Mr. Jinks, a handyman of 53 Bohemia Rd, and Pettit's, a firm of builders based at 182 Queen's Road. Elsie sent all her laundry home during her nation-wide tour and complained in 1918 that her laundress 'is hopeless! Has sent no clean combinations to wear and no stockings.'

Elsie felt driven to educate people in (conservative) politics and economics, to encourage individual responsibility and enterprise, and to oppose socialism and communism. With these ends in view she joined the newly-formed 'Women's Guild of Empire', which was eventually to boast 40,000 members in 30 branches. Elsie was secretary and edited the Guild's journal *The Bulletin* (whose slogan was: 'Women Unite to save the Nation'). The Guild believed that strikes caused misery and unemployment and that unions should keep out of politics. In 1919 Elsie was Honorary Secretary of *Deeds Not Words*, a committee formed to collect money to present to Mrs. Pankhurst and Christabel, in recognition of their great financial and personal sacrifice for the suffrage movement.

Having been so involved in political campaigns and war work, and with her large private income obviating the need to earn a wage, it was not until the age of 31 that Elsie turned her attention to a profession. She decided to become a lawyer. She could not have done this very much earlier, in any case, because until the 1919 Sex Disqualification (Removal) Act women were barred from entering most professions. It took a lot of cash, too: initially, £50 deposit and over £50 in fees was demanded. Elsie was accepted as a student by the Middle Temple in 1921 and in 1924 was one of the first women called to the Bar.[9] To have completed all the work in just three years was a magnificent achievement, prompting Elsie and Edith to take a celebratory trip to Geneva.

Elsie, based in Pump Court, practised on the South Eastern Circuit. She was the first woman barrister to appear at the Old Bailey when she won a libel action brought by the National Union of Seamen against a communist. In the mid-20s Elsie published a book, *The Law of Child Protection* and in 1928 the London *Evening Standard* printed her essay, *Why women do not write Utopias*.[10]

Elsie took a great interest in her work and joined The International Federation of Women in Legal Careers, which was founded in Paris in 1928. But in 1938 she felt another vocation calling, so she gave up law and enrolled in the brand-new, and later famous, Women's Voluntary Services (WVS). For two years she was Organiser in the Information and Public Meetings department. She then worked briefly for the Ministry of Information before spending three years in the USA as a liaison officer in the BBC Overseas Services. She resigned about 1943-45 to become Chief of General Services to the London office, responsible for conferences. In 1946 she returned to the USA to help set up the United Nations Commission on the Status of Women. Elsie was a representative of the Secretary-General, and was Chief of the Division for the Advancement of Women.[11]

After her return to England in the late 1940s, Elsie spent weekdays at her flat near the Victoria & Albert Museum[12] and, from 1951, weekends at a modest flat on the top floor of one of her properties: 25 Silchester Road, St Leonards. She had bought these properties in 1913 and converted them into flats. Edith, now 87, was in a nearby nursing home.[13] As a wealthy and powerful woman, Elsie was an unusual person to find in a working-class area of tradesmen and small shops. She was then 63, an assertive, no-nonsense woman, very stout and grey-haired. She drove an impressive black Rover car and is reputed to have once had a council parking restriction lifted because it inconvenienced her.

In Elsie's letters and other documents there is no hint of a liaison or intimate relationship with anyone. One day she told her ground floor tenants that she was having her flat refurbished because a 'close lady friend' was coming to live with her. Soon afterwards, they were shocked to find her sobbing on the stairs: her friend had died suddenly. Elsie, a woman not given to displays of emotion or weakness, was inconsolable.[14]

After her mother died in October 1953, Elsie had no further need of a home in St Leonards. She let the third flat until she sold them all in 1961 and purchased Bachelors, a country house at Cowbeech Hill, Hailsham.

During the sixties she wrote articles for Wycombe Abbey's magazine, and in 1965 produced a 95-page book about its founder Dame Frances Dove, entitled '*Stands There a School*'. She was interviewed by suffrage historian David Mitchell on 11 November 1964, and by historian Antonia Raeburn in the late sixties. She and suffragette Grace Roe were featured in the February 1975 edition of '*Calling All Women.*' She is acknowledged in Raeburn's book, *'Militant Suffragettes'*, as 'Miss Elsie Bowerman M. A. Barrister-at-Law' for relating her mother's experience in a suffragette riot.

Elsie had carried out voluntary work for the United Girls' School Mission since her schooldays. Between 1931 and 1962 she was successively treasurer, secretary and chairman of the Finance and General Purposes Committee, and was then chairman until her death. Elsie saved the Mission from closure during its years of crisis, (she once even stood in as resident warden). Thanks to her it re-emerged as the Peckham Settlement, supported by the Union of Girls' Schools for Social Service.

Throughout her life Elsie also retained her connections with Wycombe Abbey. She was a member of the school council and carried out a considerable amount of organisational work during the war to ensure the school's survival. She helped set up an endowment fund and established the Dove-Bowerman Trust, dedicated to the fortunes of Wycombe Abbey, and described it as 'the crowning work of her life'.

Elsie suffered a stroke in 1972 and died on 18th October 1973, aged 83, leaving over £143,000 - the equivalent of over a million pounds today. Her bequests reflected the things closest to her heart. £1000 went to the Chichester Cathedral Fund (to increase stipends); £500 each was left to the Seaman's Mission, Arthur Owen of Rye, and Mary Jenner of Hellingly. £200 each went to Warbleton Parish Church, the Gardeners' Benevolent Fund and the RNLI and £100 went to the Old Hastings Preservation Society. To Margaret Cousins, of Benedicts, Ardingly, she left the remainder of her possessions and the largest personal bequest: £4000. Her books, piano, music and records went to Wycombe Abbey School, as did the bulk of her estate, which she left to the school's Dove-Bowerman Trust, which is still in existence. Although her funeral was held at St Mary the Virgin, Warbleton, Elsie was buried in the family grave, along with her parents, in Hastings cemetery.

In an obituary, Miss Fisher of Wycombe Abbey wrote:

It was the vitality and the gaiety of Elsie Bowerman's spirit that captivated us and made us respond with smiles whenever she appeared in the School. Welcome everywhere, but happiest in the Cloister, she invigorated us with her penetrating comments, lively wit and clear-sighted vision.

Miss K. A. Walpole, headmistress of Wycombe Abbey, described Elsie as:

... not just an able, strong-minded woman. Determined? Yes. Impatient? Yes - with injustice and narrow-minded foolishness. But essentially she was modest, friendly, relaxed. She loved the good things of life - music above all, art, her garden; she enjoyed good food, good wine, fun, sociability. Many of us will remember her generous hospitality, a smaller number the joy of her close friendship. Her concern also reached out to all those who lived about her - her daily help, her taxi-driver, the people of the village, those with whom she worshipped in the village church.

As her life drew to its close her thoughts turned to abiding loyalties, loyalty to church, country, school and friends; though finding it hard to lose her independence because of failing strength, she rejoiced in her remembrance of a long and happy life; as ever, she looked to the future. Let the last words be hers:

"As one approaches the end of life an unaccountable feeling of melancholy creeps over one. This is not because of any fear of the life to come, rather a joyful anticipation. Life has been so full of surprises that one cannot believe that there are not even greater joys and adventures in store. Here's Au Revoir to all my friends and countless thanks for all their love and kindness which has given me such a happy life in this world - Here's to our next happy meeting in the next one.

Elsie Bowerman".

REFERENCES

[1] Property later inherited by Elsie and Edith included 2, 5 & 8 Grand Parade; 7 & 7a South St; 1 - 5 Crystal Square; 11 North St; 62 Norman Rd; 4 & 5 Castle St; 68 & 69 Marina; 9 & 19 Wellington Place; 37 London Rd. Most were shops with flats above. The shops were at 14 Robertson St (hosier), 33/35 London Rd and 9½ Castle St.

[2] According to Miss Fisher, Wycombe Abbey School.

[3] 6 Cumberland Gardens.

[4] Born 12 April 1840.

[5] Women's Social & Political Union.

[6] Dr. Elsie Inglis (1864-1916). Studied at the Edinburgh School of Medicine for Women, founded by Sophia Jex-Blake q.v.

[7] *Bath Chronicle* 7 June 1918

[8] Seventeen women stood but only one was elected, and as a Sinn Feiner she did not take her seat in the house.

[9] The first woman had been called to the Bar in 1921.

[10] *Evening Standard* 17th July 1928.

[11] Elsie's name is listed as the first Chief on the D. A. W website at www.un.org/womenwatch/daw/daw/.

[12] 22b Egerton Gardens, SW3.

[13] Belfield Nursing Home, 1, Hollington Park Rd. Matron: Miss. C V Cane. The 1950 telephone directory lists a Mrs. E. M. Chignall (sic) The Nurseries, Ridgewood, Uckfield, Sussex. Bellfield is now the Sussex Clinic.

[14] I am most indebted to Mr W Carley of St Leonards for his personal reminiscences of Elsie during the 1950s and 1960s.

MATILDA BETHAM-EDWARDS 1836~1919

If not the greatest, Miss Betham-Edwards was certainly one of the most remarkable of the group of distinguished women whom we now call Mid-Victorian.

Sarah Grand, 1919.

Matilda was born in an Elizabethan manor house in Westerfield, Suffolk and her mother died when she was 12. She was mainly self-educated and especially loved great works of literature. After a spell as a pupil-teacher in a seminary at Peckham, London, she studied German in Austria and Germany and French in Paris. She declined one offer of marriage and another to be a companion to a rich older woman, and lived alone all her life with only her servants and guests for company.

Matilda wrote more than thirty novels and twenty other publications including biography, poetry, ballads, children's stories and articles for magazines and newspapers. One of her early ballads was highly acclaimed by Charles Dickens, who paid her £5 for it and published it in his *Household Words* in 1856. His letter of praise was among her most prized possessions.

She began to write her first novel, *The White House by the Sea*, while still a teenager. This was published in 1857, became an immediate success, and remained in print for over forty years. It is revealing of the prevailing attitude to women that she once tried to make publishers believe that a novel of hers was the work of a man.

Kitty, perhaps her greatest work, was highly acclaimed by the critics. Coventry Patmore called it 'a classic' and Baron Houghton said it was the best novel he had ever read. First published in 1869, it remained in print until 1907. Matilda's *Six Life Studies of Famous Women* (1884) included a biographical sketch of her aunt and godmother, the poet Mary Matilda Betham (1776-

sketch of her aunt and godmother, the poet Mary Matilda Betham (1776-1852), and her *Mid Victorian Memories* includes a chapter on Barbara Bodichon and George Eliot.

Matilda's travel writing included *A Winter with the Swallows* (1866) and *Through Spain to the Sahara* (1867), which record her time abroad with Barbara Bodichon. The pair toured through Spain in 1866-7 before spending a few months in Algiers with Barbara's husband. Through Barbara's influence, Matilda spent 1875 living in France and on her return wrote *A Year in Western France* and, later, *The Roof of France,* which were very widely read and which led the French government to confer upon her the honour of Officier De L'Instruction Publique de France in 1891 – the first English person to receive this accolade. A lifelong francophile, she later wrote *France of Today (1892)* and *A Romance of Dijon* (1894). *Cassell's Magazine* described her work as 'painstaking, careful, honest, observant.'

In 1884 she came to live in Hastings, having inherited a fine house at 3 High Wickham from her cousin Amelia Blandford Edwards, a well-known Egyptologist. She named the house Villa Julia, after a close friend.

Villa Julia and a signed portrait of Matilda at her writing desk.

Matilda was once described as an uncompromising Radical and Nonconformist ... [who] could, on occasions, be caustic, and was always outspoken'.[1] She exhibited socialist sympathies in *The Sylvesters* (1871) and was a friend of several feminists including suffragists Mrs. Darent Harrison[2] and Miss Fricker Hall, Dr. Elizabeth Blackwell, writer Sarah Grand and Barbara Leigh Smith Bodichon. She was sufficiently interested in women's rights to sign the 1866 petition for women's suffrage but later revised her opinion and became what Sarah Grand called 'a passive opponent of the movement'.[3]

For reasons I have been unable to establish, it is nowadays claimed that Matilda was a lesbian and her poetry is included in the *Penguin Book Of Homosexual Verse* as well as on two lesbian websites. While it is true that there does not appear to have been any romantic attachment to a man, she did not seem that enamoured of women, either, accusing them of 'disloyalty, ingratitude and jealousy' towards one another. This, she asserted. 'will ever remain with me an unanswerable objection to women's political advancement'.[4]

Despite her mild opposition to the women's rights movement, Matilda was nevertheless incensed at the ingratitude shown to Barbara Bodichon for spending her life campaigning for women's rights. She wrote: 'Long ago Madame Bodichon's writings ought to have been collected, edited and published by some grateful beneficiary of her foundation (i.e. a student of Girton College). Not a bit of it!'[5] When women won the vote in 1918 she remarked,

> .. and to-day what do women not owe [Barbara Bodichon]? To one of the first, most intrepid, and most liberal advocates of parliamentary equality, at last has come posthumous equality. Let us hope that the newly enfranchised will prove themselves worthy of the privilege.[6]

In 1909 at the age of 73 she received a Gold Medal for nine volumes of work published over 35 years, which she exhibited in the Place of Women's Work in the Franco-British Exhibition of 1908. In her later years she was described as 'a typical English gentlewoman of the old school'.[7] She suffered a stroke in 1919, after which she became something of a recluse, admitting only Sarah Grand and Mrs. Darent Harrison. When she died, her book *Mid Victorian Memories* was in the process of being published. Her fame at that time is evidenced by the long obituary she warranted in *The Times*. In 1920, a plaque was placed on her house, which is now a Grade II listed building.

Some of Matilda's books are available on the Internet from antiquarian book specialists in the USA. Her 46-page *Snow Flakes and the Stories They Told the Children* is currently priced at $250.

REFERENCES

[1] Kernahan, C. (1923) *Celebrities*.

[2] Mrs. Darent Harrison was a friend of Elsie Bowerman's mother, Edith Bowerman Chibnall.

[3] Betham Edwards, M. (1919) *Mid Victorian Memories*, p.xxxi.

[4] Betham Edwards, M. (1919) *Mid Victorian Memories*, p.67

[5] ibid.

[6] ibid.

[7] Ibid.

A COMPENDIUM OF VISITORS

QUEEN ADELAIDE (1792-1849)

Adelaide was the wife of King William IV and aunt of Queen Victoria. She and the King's sister, Princess Augusta, stayed at a house in Seymour Place, St Leonards in October 1837. She had recently been widowed and had also lost two of her children. As well as this, she was ill, and had come to recuperate. Local dignitaries planned a huge reception but she specifically requested that no fuss and no ceremony be made. However, a band played right in front of her house and special gas illuminations spelt her initials in glorious colours. Her address was published in the local guide book and a crowd of about 3,000 people gathered to see her. She was not amused.

The Dowager Queen had an income of £100,000 a year. She contributed to several local charities, donated 20 guineas (£21) towards a Holdich pipe-organ for St Leonards Church and paid for a reserved pew at St Mary-in-the-Castle Church.

The royal party stayed until February 1838. The Queen's visit is memorialised in name by the *Queen Adelaide* public house, West Street, Hastings, and Seymour Place was renamed Adelaide Place and is now part of Grand Parade. The house, now no. 23, bears a commemorative plaque.

HERTHA MARKS AYRTON (1854-1923)

Physicist. A friend and protégée of Barbara Bodichon, Hertha Marks was a frequent visitor to Hastings. She was educated at Girton, the college co-founded by Barbara, and was a brilliant physicist. Hertha was the first woman elected to the Institution of Electrical Engineers and in 1902 was nominated for fellowship of the Royal Society, but this was refused because she was a married woman. In 1906 she received the Society Hughes Medal. She and her daughter Barbara were militant suffragettes.

Hertha Ayrton

Jane Carlyle

The Duchess of
Kent and Princess
Victoria

George Eliot

Mary Howitt

Anna Kingsford

Adelaide Anne Procter

Lizzie Siddal

The Duchess of
Gloucester

ANNIE WOOD BESANT (1847–1933)

Social reformer. While living with her mother in Warrior Square she married Frank Besant at St Mary Magdalen Church on 21st December 1867. Among many other things she was a Theosophist and an advocate of birth control, socialism, and Indian home rule.

CATHERINE BOOTH (1829-1890)

Co-founder of, and preacher in the Salvation Army. Drew a massive crowd when she preached in Hastings in 1874.

LADY BOOTHBY (1812-1858)

Comedy actress. Born Louisa Macnamara, she used the stage name Mordaunt. In 1829 she married John Nisbett, who died in 1832. She returned to the London stage until her marriage to Sir William Boothby in 1844. He died two years later and she acted again until her retirement in 1851. After visiting friends at Quarry Castle for many years, in 1846 she purchased Rosemount, Quarry Hill (now demolished), and later had the house altered to accommodate a private theatre. She was a member and participant of the Queen's St Leonards Archers.

MRS PATRICK CAMPBELL (1865-1940)

Celebrated actress. Visited Hastings many times.

JANE WELSH CARLYLE (1801-1866)

Writer and wife of the historian Thomas Carlyle. Visited St Leonards from March to July 1864, staying 8 weeks with Dr Peyton Blakiston at 5 Wellington Square before taking a house at 117 Marina. Jane's account of these lodgings is unusual, since St Leonards prided itself on the high quality of its accommodation.

> The house was new, clean, light enough, and well aired; otherwise paltry in the extreme - small, misbuilt every inch of it; a despicable, cockney, scamped edifice; a rickety bandbox rather than a house. But that did not much concern us, tenants only for a month or two - nay, withal there were traces that the usual inhabitants (two old ladies, probably very poor) had been cleanly, neat persons, sensible, as we, of the sins and miseries of their scamped, despicable dwelling-place, poor, good souls!
>
> Hastings, St. Leonards, Battle, Rye, Winchelsea, Beachy Head, intrinsically all a beautiful region (when not cockneyfied, and turned to

cheap and nasty chaos and the mortar tubs), and yet in the world is no place I should so much shudder to see again.[1]

Her husband also stayed there, and completed his famous biography *Frederick the Great* on the premises. The house now boasts a Blue Plaque in his memory.

ELIZA CARTE (1815-1885)

Mother of Richard D' Oyly Carte, who was responsible for promoting Gilbert & Sullivan's comic operas in his London theatres. Taking a short break from London, Eliza and her husband took the train to Hastings on 24th January 1885, where she booked into lodgings at 92 High Street. However, her holiday was to be a short one: after a shopping trip that day, she died of heart failure at 6.30pm.

CLARA COLLETT M. A. (1860-1948)

Feminist and social economist. A frequent visitor.

GEORGE ELIOT (Marian Evans) (1819-1880)

Novelist. Friend of Barbara Bodichon, stayed at Hastings in May 1845 and St Leonards in 1846 and 1854.

BEATRICE HARRADEN (1864-1936)

Novelist and suffragette. At one time lived in Hastings. Wrote a best-seller entitled *Ships that Pass in the Night* (1893).

ELLEN JULIA HOLLOND (1822-1884)

Traveller, author and philanthropist. Wrote *A Lady's Journal of Her Travels in Egypt and Nubia (1858-9)* in 1864.

MARY HOWITT (1799-1888)

Writer and poet. She married William Howitt in 1821 and they became Unitarians in the 1840s. She supported the Anti-Corn Law League and anti-slavery movements, and worked as editor of periodicals such as *Howitt's Journal*, and *The People's Journal*. Mary Howitt participated actively in the abolitionism of the 1840s and 1850s, and helped to organise the petition for reform of married women's property legislation. Lived in Hastings in the 1840s-50s. Bessie Rayner Parkes recalled: 'It was [in Hastings] in 1846-7, that I first heard of the Howitts as a family. Mrs. Howitt's tales and poems

---

[1] Carlyle, T (ed.) (1883) *Letters & Memorials of Jane Welsh Carlyle*, Longmans, Green & Co, London, p198

had, of course, been familiar to me from early childhood, more especially the exquisite "Sketches from Natural History," containing that ballad beginning "Will you walk into my parlour, said the Spider to the Fly," which has become so much a classic phrase that I have seen it quoted in prose in a political leader, without any reference to the authoress, or to the fact that the quotation formed part of a verse'.

Dr. ANNA KINGSFORD (1846-1888)

Feminist and Theosophist. Anna Kingsford (née Bonus) was a woman of high achievement for the betterment of humanity. When she was a teenager, Anna's family moved to 56 Warrior Square. With her mother, Anna took part in archery competitions with the Queen's St Leonards Archers, winning a bouquet for best shot in the gold in 1863. On her father's death, in 1865, she inherited an annual income of £700. In November 1867 while collecting signatures in Hastings in support of the Married Women's Property Act she met Miss F. J. Theobald, who later introduced her to spiritualism. A month later, Anna married her cousin, the Reverend Algernon Kingsford, on the condition that she could pursue her own interests. The wedding took place at St Mary Magdalen Church on 31 December, 1867. On her honeymoon she became ill (she was asthmatic) and returned to Warrior Square, where her daughter Eadith was born in 1868.
In January 1869 she attended a seance at Miss Theobald's in Hastings. In 1872 Anna was co-organiser and speaker at Hastings' first women's suffrage meeting. She wrote to both Hastings MPs asking them to support women's suffrage in a forthcoming vote, but they refused. As a married woman, Anna left St Leonards for her husband's parish at Atcham, near Shrewsbury. It was an unusual marriage as Anna frequently lived apart from her husband.
Anna was among the pioneer women doctors, for she qualified in medicine in 1880. She was against vivisection, and was a pioneer vegetarian. While in Hastings in 1882 she attended at least one meeting of the Philosophical Society: it is minuted that, as a woman, she was forbidden to read out her paper on anti-vivisection. The (male) secretary offered to read it our for her, but Anna declined. She edited the *Lady's Own Paper*, and campaigned for women's rights and women's suffrage. In 1883 Anna became President of the British Theosophical Society and in 1884 co-founded the Hermetic Society. Among her various writings *The Perfect Way or the Finding of Christ* and *Clothed in the Sun* stand out as classics in the esoteric and mystic field.

ANNA M McNEILL WHISTLER(?-1881)

Anna was the figure in the famous portrait *Arrangement in Grey and Black No 1*, better known as *Whistler's Mother*. She lived and died at Talbot House, 43 St Mary's Terrace. Anna was a devout Christian, and her artist son James so admired her that in his early manhood he exchanged his middle name 'Abbott' for her maiden name 'McNeill'.

BEATRIX POTTER (1866-1943)

Stayed at 3 Robertson Terrace in 1903, where she wrote two stories. Illustrations for *The Tale of Little Pig Robinson* (1930) were based on the Net Huts in Hastings' fishing quarter.

ADELAIDE ANNE PROCTER (1825-1864)

Author, hymn-writer, poet and feminist, who lived in Hastings in the mid-1800s. Under the pen-name Mary Berwick, her verse was first published in Dicken's *Household Words* in 1853 and five years later she published a two-volume collection of poetry, *Legends and Lyrics*. Adelaide was a lifelong feminist and was a student of Queen's College for Ladies. She served on two Social Science Association committees on women's work, and joined with Barbara Bodichon to found the Society for Promoting the Employment of Women. She donated the proceeds of the sales of her successful poetry anthology *A Chaplet of Verse* to a night-refuge for homeless women. Her poetry was once as popular as that of Tennyson, though she is most famous for writing the words to *The Lost Chord*, to which Sir Arthur Sullivan wrote the music.

OLIVE SCHREINER (1855-1920)

Novelist and feminist. A South African, Olive spent many winters in St Leonards between October 1882 and 1899. She stayed at 4 Robertson Terrace and (more often) at the Edinburgh House Hotel.[2] She attended meetings of the local branch of the Women's Suffrage Society and wrote *Women and Labour*. Her most famous book was *The Story of an African Farm*.

ELIZABETH SIDDAL (1829-1862)

Artist and model. Friend of Barbara Bodichon. In 1855 she stayed for 10 weeks at 5 High Street and returned in 1860 to marry Dante Gabriel Rossetti at St Clement's Church.

PRINCESS SOPHIA MATILDA of GLOUCESTER (1773-1844)

Stayed for three months at Bohemia House before moving in 1831 to North Villa, later named Gloucester Lodge, Maze Hill. She was a daughter of the Prince of Wales and a niece of King George III. She never married.

---

[2] Later the Marlborough Hotel, now demolished.

CAROLINE FRY (WILSON) (1787- 1846)

Writer of romantic and religious poetry, including *Christ Our Law, Poetical Catechism , Serious Poetry* and *The Listener.* Friend of Mary Howitt. Lived at 2 London Road (above the Saxon Shades beer-shop) and Beach Cottages. Was frequently seen on the Parade wearing a man's hat and cloth pelisse.

QUEEN VICTORIA (1819-1901)

Although she and her mother, the Duchess of Kent, visited Hastings for day trips from Tunbridge Wells in 1826 and 1827, Victoria's only sojourn here was as a 15-year-old Princess when she and her mother stayed in St Leonards for almost three months during the winter of 1834-5 with her governess Baroness Lehzen, and Lady Flora Hastings.

On their arrival at Ore they were greeted by the Mayor and travelled through several triumphal arches of laurels and flowers. They were accompanied to St Leonards by crowds of townspeople walking alongside, while houses en route were decorated with flowers and ribbons. It was said that 20,000 people were at St Leonards to greet them. A red cloth was laid from the carriage to the front door of 57 Marina, then called Victoria House (now Crown House), the home provided for them by James Burton. Later the ladies received a gift of a dish of fresh fish, delivered with great ceremony by six local fishermen, accompanied by a marching band. Fireworks completed the welcome. The remainder of their visit was beset by numerous unpleasant incidents, tragedies and accidents.

For the rest of her life, Victoria never again visited Hastings. This has been the subject of speculation by various historians. Perhaps she disapproved of her Aunt Adelaide's wishes (see above) being ignored. Victoria passed through Hastings on her way elsewhere in 1855, and while the train swapped engines she was treated to a brief civic reception by the Mayor. She was also waved at as she passed by in a steamboat in 1858. A bronze statue of Queen Victoria, erected in 1902, stands at Warrior Square, looking out to sea. The bullet hole at her knee was the work of a Nazi gunner during the Second World War.

A great-great-great-grandchild of Queen Victoria, Helene Sophie van Eyck, was married in Hastings in January 1986 to Roderick Harman. Their two daughters were born at St Leonards in 1986 and 1989.

Olive Schreiner   Annie Besant   Catherine Booth   Caroline Fry

APPENDIX 1: Excerpts from *A Brief Summary in Plain Language of the Most Important Laws Concerning Women; Together with a Few Observations Thereon* (1854) by Barbara Leigh Smith Bodichon

LAWS CONCERNING WOMEN.

LEGAL CONDITION OF UNMARRIED WOMEN OR SPINSTERS.

A single woman.
A SINGLE woman has the same rights to property, to protection from the law, and has to pay the same taxes to the State, as a man.

No political franchise.
Yet a woman of the age of twenty-one, having the requisite property qualifications, cannot vote in elections for members of Parliament.

Has a parochial vote.
A woman duly qualified can vote upon parish questions, and for parish officers, overseers, surveyors, vestry clerks, &c.

Heiress.
If her father or mother die intestate (i.e., without a will) she takes an equal share with her brothers and sisters of the personal property i.e., goods, chattels, moveables), but her eldest brother, if she have one, and his children, even daughters, will take the real property, (i.e., not personal property, but all other, as land, &c.), as the heir-at-law; males and their issue being preferred to females; if, however, she have sisters only, then all the sisters take the real property equally. If she be an only child, she is entitled to all the intestate real and personal property.

No public employments.
The church and nearly all offices under government are closed to women. The Post-office affords some little employment to them; but there is no important office which they can hold, with the single exception of that of Sovereign.

The professions of law and medicine, whether or not closed by law, are closed in fact. They may engage in trade, and may occupy inferior situations, such as matron of a charity, sextoness of a church, and a few parochial offices are open to them. Women are occasionally governors of prisons for women, overseers of the poor, and parish clerks. A woman may be ranger of a park; a woman can take part in the government of a great empire by buying East India Stock.

...

Seduction.
If a woman is seduced, she has no remedy against the seducer; nor has her father, excepting as he is considered in law as being her master and she his servant, and the seducer as having deprived him of her services. Very slight service is deemed sufficient in law, but evidence of some service is absolutely necessary, whether the daughter be of full age or under age.

These are the only special laws concerning single women: the law speaks of men only, but women are affected by all the laws and incur the same responsibilities in all their contracts and doings as men.

LAWS CONCERNING MARRIED WOMEN.

...

Married women no legal existence.

A man and wife are one person in law; the wife loses all her rights as a single woman, and her existence is entirely absorbed in that of her husband. He is civilly responsible for her acts; she lives under his protection or cover, and her condition is called coverture.

A husband has a right to the person of his wife. A woman's body belongs to her husband; she is in his custody, and he can enforce his right by a writ of habeas corpus.

Her personal property becomes his.

What was her personal property before marriage, such as money in hand, money at the bank, jewels, household goods, clothes, &c., becomes absolutely her husband's, and he may assign or dispose of them at his pleasure whether he and his wife live together or not.

He takes her chattels real.

A wife's chattels real (i.e., estates held during a term of years, or the next presentation to a church living, &c.) become her husband's by his doing some act to appropriate them; but, if the wife survives, she resumes her property.

Equity.

Equity is defined to be a correction or qualification of the law, generally made in the part wherein it faileth, or is too severe. In other words, the correction of that wherein the law, by reason of its universality, is deficient. While the Common Law gives the whole of a wife's personal property to her husband, the Courts of Equity, when he proceeds therein to recover property in right of his wife, oblige him to make a settlement of some portion of it upon her, if she be unprovided for and virtuous. If her property be under £200, or £10 a year, a Court of Equity will not interpose.

Her right to support.

Neither the Courts of Common Law nor Equity have any direct power to oblige a man to support his wife,--the Ecclesiastical Courts (i.e. Courts
held by the Queen's authority as governor of the Church, for matters which chiefly concern religion) and a Magistrate's court at the instance of her parish alone can do this.

His power over her real property.

A husband has a freehold estate in his wife's lands during the joint existence of himself and his wife, that is to say, he has absolute possession of them as long as they both live. If the wife dies without children, the property goes to his heir, but if she has borne a child, her husband holds possession until his death.

A married woman's earnings not her own but her husband's.

Money earned by a married woman belongs absolutely to her husband; that and all sources of income, excepting those mentioned above, are included in the term personal property.

A wife's will.

By the particular permission of her husband she can make a will of her personal property, for by such a permission he gives up his right. But he may revoke his permission at any time before probate (i.e. the exhibiting and proving a will before the Ecclesiastical Judge having jurisdiction over the place where the party died).

A mother's rights over children.

The legal custody of children belongs to the father. During the life-time of a sane father, the mother has no rights over her children, except a limited power over infants, and the father may take them from her and dispose of them as he thinks fit.

If there be a legal separation of the parents, and there be neither agreement nor order of the Court, giving the custody of the children to either parent, then the right to the custody of the children (except for the nutriment of infants) belongs legally to the father.

Responsibility of a wife.

A married woman cannot sue or be sued for contracts nor can she enter into contracts except as the agent of her husband; that is to say, her word alone is not binding in law, and persons giving a wife credit have no remedy against her. There are some exceptions, as where she contracts debts upon estates settled to her separate use, or where a wife carries on trade separately, according to the custom of London, &c.

Responsibility of a husband

A husband is liable for his wife's debts contracted before marriage, and also for her breaches of trust committed before marriage.

Witnesses.

Neither a husband nor a wife can be witnesses against one another in criminal cases, not even after the death or divorce of either.

Wife cannot bring actions.

A wife cannot bring actions unless the husband's name is joined.

A wife acts under coercion of her husband.

As the wife acts under the command and control of her husband, she is excused from punishment for certain offences, such as theft, burglary, housebreaking, &c., if committed in his presence and under his influence. A wife cannot be found guilty of concealing her felon husband or of concealing a felon jointly with her husband. She cannot be found guilty of stealing from her husband or of setting his house on fire, as they are one person in law. A husband and wife cannot be found guilty of conspiracy, as that offence cannot be committed unless there are two persons.

USUAL PRECAUTIONS AGAINST THE LAWS CONCERNING PROPERTY OF MARRIED WOMEN.

An engaged woman cannot dispose of her property. When a woman has consented to a proposal of marriage, she cannot dispose or give away her property without the knowledge of her betrothed; if she make any such disposition without his knowledge, even if he be ignorant of the existence of her property, the disposition will not be legal.

Settlements.

It is usual, before marriage, in order to secure a wife and her children against the power of the husband, to make with his consent a settlement of some property on the wife, or to make an agreement before marriage that a settlement shall be made after marriage. It is in the power of the Court of Chancery to enforce the performance of such agreements.

Differences between Common Law and Equity.

Although the Common Law does not allow a married woman to possess any property, yet in respect of property settled for her separate use, Equity endeavours to treat her as a single woman.

She can acquire such property by contract before marriage with her husband, or by gift from him or other persons.

There are great difficulties and complexities in making settlements, and they should always be made by a competent lawyer.

Indictment for theft.

When a wife's property is stolen, the property (legally belonging to the husband) must be laid as his in the indictment.

SEPARATION AND DIVORCE.

A husband and wife can separate upon a deed containing terms for their immediate separation, but they cannot legally agree to separate at a future time. The trustees of the wife must be parties to the deed, and agree with the husband as to what property the wife is to take, for a husband and wife cannot convenant together.

Divorce is of two kinds:-
1st. Divorce à mensa et thoro, being only a separation from bed and board.
2nd. Divorce à vinculo matrimonii, being an entire dissolution of the bonds of matrimony.

The grounds for the first kind of divorce are, 1st. Adultery, 2nd. Intolerable Cruelty, and 3rd. Unnatural Practices. The Ecclesiastical Courts can do no more than pronounce for this first kind of divorce, or rather separation, as the matrimonial tie is not severed, and there is always a possibility of reconciliation. The law cannot dissolve a lawful marriage; it is only in the Legislature that this power is vested. It requires an act of Parliament to constitute a divorce à vinculo matrimonii, but the investigation rests by usage with the Lords alone, the House of Commons acting upon the faith that the House of Lords came to a just conclusion.

This divorce is pronounced on account of adultery in the wife, and in some cases of aggravated adultery on the part of the husband.

The expenses of only a common divorce bill are between six hundred and seven hundred pounds, which makes the possibility of release from the matrimonial bond a privilege of the rich.

A wife cannot be a plaintiff, defendant, or witness in an important part of the proceeding for a divorce, which evidently must lead to much injustice.

LAWS CONCERNING A WIDOW.

Her property.

A widow recovers her real property, but if there be a settlement she is restricted by its provisions. She recovers her chattels real if her husband has not disposed of them by will or otherwise.

A wife's paraphernalia.

A wife' paraphernalia (i.e., her clothes and ornaments) which her husband owns during his lifetime, and which his creditors can seize for his debts, becomes her property on his death.

Her liabilities.

A widow is liable for any debts which she contracted before marriage, and which have been left unpaid during her marriage.

A widow is not bound to bury her dead husband, it being the duty of his legal representative.

A widow's one-third.

If a man die intestate, the widow, if there are children, is entitled to one-third of the personality; if there are no children, to one-half: the other is distributed among the next of kin, among whom the widow is not counted. If there is no next of kin the moiety goes to the crown. The husband can, of course, by will deprive a wife of all right in the personality.

Quarantine.

A right is granted in Magna Charta to a widow to remain forty days in her husband's house after his death, provided she do not marry during that time.

Dower.

A widow has a right to a third of her husband's lands and tenements for her life. Right of dower is generally superseded by settlements giving the wife a jointure. If she accept a jointure she has no claim to dower.

LAWS CONCERNING ILLEGITIMATE CHILDREN AND THEIR MOTHERS.

Maintenance.

A single woman having a child may throw the maintenance upon the putative father, so called to distinguish him from a husband, until the age of thirteen.

The law only enforces the parents to maintain such child, and the sum the father is obliged to pay, after an order of affiliation is proved against him, never exceeds two shillings and sixpence a week.

The mother, as long as she is unmarried or a widow, is bound to maintain such child as a part of her family until such child attain the age of sixteen.

A man marrying a woman having a child or children at the time of such marriage is bound to support them, whether legitimate or not, until the age of sixteen.

…

REMARKS.

THESE are the principal laws concerning women.

Philosophical thinkers have generally come to the conclusion that the tendency of progress is gradually to dispense with law,--that is to say, as each individual man becomes unto himself a law, less external restraint is necessary. And certainly the most urgently needed reforms are simple erasures from the statute book. Women, more than any other members of the community, suffer from over-legislation.

A woman of twenty-one becomes an independent human creature, capable of holding and administering property to any amount; or, if she can earn money, she may appropriate her earnings freely to any purpose she thinks good. Her father has no power over her or her property. But if she unites herself to a man, the law immediately steps in, and she finds herself legislated for, and her condition of life suddenly and entirely changed. Whatever age she may be of, she is again considered as an infant,--she is again under "reasonable restraint,"--she loses her separate existence, and is merged in that of her husband.

"In short," says Judge Hurlbut, "a woman is courted and wedded as an angel, and yet denied the dignity of a rational and moral being ever after."

…

Truly "she hath lost her streame," she is absorbed, and can hold nothing of herself, she has no legal right to any property; not even her clothes, books, and household goods are her own, and any money which she earns can be robbed from her legally by her husband, nay, even after the commencement of a treaty of marriage she cannot dispose of her own property without the knowledge of her betrothed. If she should do so, it is deemed a fraud in law and can be set aside after marriage as an injury to her husband.

It is always said, even by those who support the existing law, that it is in fact never acted upon by men of good feeling. That is true; but the very admission condemns the law, and it is not right that the good feeling of men should be all that a woman can look to for simple justice.

There is now a large and increasing class of women who gain their own livelihood, and the abolition of the laws which give husbands this unjust power is most urgently needed.

Rich men and fathers might still make what settlements they pleased, and appoint trustees for the protection of minors and such women as needed protection; but we imagine it well proved that the principle of protection is wrong, and that the education of freedom and responsibility will enable women to take better care of themselves and others too than can be insured to them by any legal precautions.

Upon women of the labouring classes the difficulty of keeping and using their own earnings presses most hardly. In that rank of life where the support of the family depends often on the joint earnings of husband and wife, it is indeed cruel that the earnings of both should be in the hands of one, and not even in the hands of that one who has naturally the strongest desire to promote the welfare of the children. All who are familiar with the working classes know how much suffering and privation is caused by the exercise of this right by drunken and bad men. It is true that men are legally bound to support their wives and children, but this does not compensate women for the loss of their moral right to their own property and earnings, nor for the loss of the mental development and independence of character gained by the possession and thoughtful appropriation of money; nor, it must be remembered, can the claim to support be enforced on the part of the wife unless she appeals to a court of law. Alas, how much will not a woman endure before she will publicly plead for a maintenance!

Why, we ask, should there be this difference between the married and unmarried condition of women? And why does marriage make so little legal difference to men, and such a mighty legal difference to women?

...

Since all the unmarried women in England are supported either by their own exertions or by the exertions or bequests of their fathers and relations, there is no reason why upon marriage they should be thrown upon the pecuniary resources of their husbands, except in so far as the claims of a third party--children--may lessen the wife's power of earning money, at the same time that it increases her expenses. Of course a woman may, and often does, by acting as housekeeper and manager of her husband's concerns, earn a maintenance and a right to share in his property, independent of any children which may come of the marriage. But it is evident that daughters ought to have some sure provision-- either a means of gaining their own bread, or property--as it is most undesirable that they should look upon marriage as a means of livelihood.

Fathers seldom feel inclined to trust their daughters' fortunes in the power of a husband, and, in the appointment of trustees, partially elude the law by a legal device. Also, the much abused Court of Chancery tried to palliate the Common Law, and recognizes a separate interest between husband and wife, and allows the wife alone to file a bill to recover and protect her property, and trustees are not necessary if there has been an agreement.

Why should not these legal devices be done away with, by the simple abolition of a law which we have outgrown?

We do not say that these laws of property are the only unjust laws concerning women to be found in the short summary which we have given, but they form a simple, tangible, and not offensive point of attack.

THE EDUCATION OF WOMEN
BY ESCULAPIUS (Barbara Leigh-Smith)
From the *Hastings & St Leonards News*, 28 July 1848

Women, in the ordinary cant of the day, are supposed to have a mission. They are not the human creature itself, but attendants sent in some way to refine and elevate man. They are supposed to be a sort of abstract of the moral and artistic principle of the world, and the prominent appearance of intellect is thought to mar the impression.

It is said that, to be perfect, women have no need of intellect in its ordinary sense. They may, (if possible) possess an intuitive knowledge of many things, but the labor of acquirement is not necessary or ought never to be shewn. That is to say, they are supposed to be somewhat angelic in their capacities or duties. Now, let us examine this. I am inclined to grant that our conception of the angelic nature scarcely includes a prominence of intellect, in the active state: The angels, who, as far as they concern us, are guardian angels, are supposed to know all relative to their office without effort; their mission is to the human heart, and the secrets of chemistry can be of no importance to them. They are above the restless searching of man; they have no need of it.

Now, I farther grant, that there is something exceedingly sweet and lofty in this conception; tenderness of grace, and tranquil power are there; not a feather is ruffled on the angels' wings; not a frown darkens their serene eyes. Were it true that women possessed this nature, I would not so much object to the life of seclusion and excessive refinement they lead. But the truth is, they are not angels by nature, and their life cannot produce the angelic constitution. Here and there we meet a woman in whom sweetness and moral dignity suffice to render her the beloved of all beholders, - such are the creations of many poets and painters; but to pretend that feminine nature in general exemplifies these charms in a sufficient degree, is an absurd lie; and any attempt to curtail an energetic vehement soul into this mould, is as vain as it would be to plant an acorn in a greenhouse pot, and call it a rose. No effort of human art can transform the one into the other, or produce from the poor acorn anything but a miserable sickly dwarf, ever engaged in a vain struggle to attain its rightful stature.

Women are not angels. In the present state of society they are frequently gossips, backbiters, idlers, fretful, unreasonable, extravagant: how many men have not a female relative combining two or more of these amiable propensities? "Talk to women and children" is, as Miss Fuller observes, a common expression. Women are not angels, as most men know to their cost; therefore let them cultivate the human faculties that in them lie, and be charming according to their endowments. Let the ideal woman receive her due share of homage. She must, for she inevitably subdues all hearts; but let your "blue" daughter, your political wife, your artistic sister, and eccentric cousin, pursue their paths unmolested, - you will never make ideals of them; you will only make your home the scene of suppressed energies and useless powers.

ESCULAPIUS
London, 1848

Appendix 2: Excerpts from *Recollections of a Happy Life* (1893), by Marianne North.

CHAPTER XIV

SOUTH AFRICA, 1882-83

ALL the continents of the world had some sort of representation in my gallery except Africa, and I resolved to begin painting there without loss of time. In August 1882 I left Dartmouth in the Grantully Castle, a ship historically famed for having once been lent by its owner, Sir Donald Currie, to Mr. Gladstone, for a trip which restored the Prime Minister to health. It took me to the Cape in rather more than eighteen days - one of the shortest voyages ever made. The first and last days of the voyage were exceedingly cold - so cold that my fingers became almost too stiff to go on with the embroidery task I had set myself to do. I had traced the pattern from a carved wooden door in the museum at Lahore, and had it transferred on gold-coloured satin-cloth, hoping to finish one side of the portière on my way to the Cape. But the ship went too quickly for me, and about half a foot of its length remained unworked when I landed--to the captain's great delight, who said he had beaten me in the race. We only stayed three hours at Madeira, and had fine weather all the way.

There was much lamentation on board when those going to Natal were told that they must not land, or they would be subject to quarantine. The pilot-boat brought out one letter only, and that was for myself; and as soon as the ship touched the shore at Cape Town, two friends met me, and put me and my boxes into a hansom-cab. One of them took me all the way out to Wynberg, seven and a half miles, round the western side of the Table Mountain, whose grand crags came down within a few hundred yards of the road, with groves of European fir-trees, oaks, and fruit-orchards, the ground under them covered with white arums, wherever the soil was moist. Near the road was a succession of pretty, unpretentious villas and cottages, in gardens more or less wild. Australian gums, wattles, and casuarinas were in full bloom, and perfectly at home there. On the sandy flats between the road and the sea were myriads of small flowers: oxalis of most dazzling pink; yellow, white, and lilac heaths, bulbs of endless variety, gazanias, and different mesembryanthemums. Mrs. Brounger, a most beautiful old lady with silver hair, gave me two rooms in her nice large old Dutch house. Her daughter, Mrs. Gamble, lived close by with her pretty children. Our meals were taken in either house alternately, both husbands being away at Government work.

Mrs. Gamble and I had many delightful drives with an old pony, which had a most remarkable talent for standing still. We used to drive him off the road into the thick bush and leave him there for hours, while we rambled about after flowers. The extraordinary novelty and variety of the different species struck me almost as much as it did at Albany in Western Australia, and there was a certain family likeness between them. But the proteas were the great wonder, and quite startled me at first. I had not formed an idea of their size and abundance: deep cups formed of waxy pointed bracts, some white, some red or pink, or tipped with colour, and fringed some with brown or black plush, others with black or white ostrich feathers. These gorgeous flower-bracts were bigger than the largest tulips, and filled with thickly packed flowers. One large variety seemed to carry its stamens outside. While painting it, I saw them begin to dance, and out came a big green beetle. I cut the flower open, and found an ants' nest. The energetic little creatures had pushed the stamens out to make room for their colony. I found all the other flowers of that kind possessed by ants, and in every nest a beetle. The young shoots generally sprang from below the flower-stalk of the protea, so that when the cone which succeeded it became ripe, it was protected and half hidden by three leafy branchlets.

Many of the species have their male flowers and cones on separate trees; like the silver tree, which only grows on the spurs of Table Mountain, where there are many groves of it, shining like real silver in the setting sunlight. It grows about twenty feet high, shaped like a fir-tree, with its flowers like balls of gold filigree at the ends of the branches. Every bit of it is lovely, but the most fascinating part is the cone, when it opens and the seeds come out with their four feathered wings, to which the seed hangs by a fine thread half an inch long. Another species of protea resembles the waratah (Grevillea) of Australia. One of them is the "krippel boom," a thick bush with a rich yellow flower at the end of each leafy branch, on which the long-tailed honeysuckers delight to perch and take their suppers, plunging in their curved beaks, and tearing the flowers all to pieces in the process. The hills were covered with low bushes, heaths, sundews, geraniums, gladioluses, lobelias, salvias, babianas, and other bulbs, daisies growing into trees, purple broom, polygalas, tritomas, and crimson velvet hyobanche.

Many friends collected for me, and two baths stood in my painting-room full of wonders. The difficulty was to make up my mind what to do first. It was impossible to paint fast enough, but we can all work hard at what we like best. Miss Robinson, the Governor's daughter, called the first day after I arrived, in her riding-habit, at ten o'clock, and told me she had been dancing at one o'clock, up and off to the meet at three, had had a glorious run, and her fingers nearly pulled off her hands by her horse. She wanted me to move into Government House, but I knew when I was well off, and declined the honour. My quieter home suited my particular work best. Indeed, I only went three times into Cape Town during the whole of my stay in South Africa. The Botanic Gardens are fine, but people there were so very economical (owing probably to the many expenses of the late useless war) that they hardly allowed enough money to keep the plants watered, and Professor Macowan, its agreeable director, was in despair about it. The museum is also an interesting collection. Mr. Trimen took me over it himself. He showed me water-birds with great red beaks, which can open oysters and eat them; also one which catches locusts on the wing, cutting off their legs and arms, dropping them as it flies, and swallowing their nutritious bodies. In the streets I saw baskets of penguins' eggs, which the Malays were buying and eating. The shells were a very blue white.

I had luncheon with the Governor, who offered to send me in a war-ship to seek the welwitschia. I did not feel sure he really meant it, and I made out that it would have to take me over a thousand miles and back in order to get to living specimens; even then there would be difficulties in going overland to find them. I thought it was asking too much of Government good-nature, but was sorry afterwards that I did not keep him to his word, as it was actually published in Nature that I had been so sent. Miss Duckett, who managed the great old Dutch farm of Groote Post in the absence of her brother in England, wrote and invited me to come and see her, and on the 7th of September I went by rail to Malmesbury.

The mountain looked glorious from the other side of the flats, all wrapped up in the morning mists, and the flats themselves were covered with gay masses of colour interspersed with patches of white sand. I had two changes of train, and found a covered country cart with four horses waiting at the end of the line, and a Boer to drive them, who only talked bad Dutch, and never took his pipe out of his mouth; but he was most willing to laugh at anything or nothing. A clever little boy of ten helped him, stopping him occasionally to run after and knock down young birds, which he put into the man's big pockets alive. He said he was going to put them in a cage. He also got a curious hanging nest of the yellow finch, and filled it with bluish eggs from other nests, which he meant to string and hang up to look pretty, he said. Whenever he liked he stopped, but I was not allowed to stop when I liked; and the new flowers which I saw and longed for were pooh-poohed! My driver was a true Boer.

The gazanias were marvellous, all turning their eyes to the sun. Looking west, all was blazing with gold and orange; looking east, I only saw the dull green backs. There were miles of the Cryptostemma calendulacea, which Australians call the African weed.

Mesembryanthemums, portulacas, ixias and babianas were also in great quantities, and of every possible tint. One of the latter flowers surpassed any I have ever seen for richness, the deepest ultramarine blue with crimson centre, and growing so close to the white or salmon-tinted sand made it shine the more. Another was of a lovely claret colour, another pink or white. The vermilion and geranium-tinted sparaxis were most gaudy, and there were small white stars with rose-tinted backs to three of their petals, which only opened at sunset; these were most delicately fragrant: also small green and drab gladioluses. All these were growing on a high plain like the Wiltshire Downs or the country about Stonehenge, with great crops of corn, every now and then terribly bad roads, and a frightful wind.

We only passed two isolated farms all the twenty miles' drive to Groote Post, a most comfortable old place, with round gable-ends, and double flight of steps leading to the upper floor, where the living-rooms were. Miss D. had meant me to come a week later, as eight ladies were already staying on a visit, but they all said they did not mind it, and gave me their best room. She had put no date but Wednesday, and said the flowers would all be over if I put it off, so I gave up the work I was doing and came at once. She was a regular Queen Bess or Boadicea for ruling men, and had no small work to do on that farm. Every morning she gave out over 100 rations of bread, meat, spirit, etc. Every morning a sheep was killed, and every week a bullock. When she heard that smallpox had broken out in the mission-station three miles off, she established a strict quarantine, and asked a neighbouring doctor what he would vaccinate her people for. He said he could not do it for less than ten shillings each, so she had herself and her niece operated on, then ordered all her people to be collected in the barn, and herself vaccinated every man, woman, and child. I tell the tale as she told it, and the result: no one had the smallpox at Groote Post.

She had the queerest collection of servants there, and some little creatures to wait at the table who were black as coals, full of fun and games behind the door. They were great mimics, and took off all our peculiarities behind our backs. I caught one of them pretending to paint in a pair of straw spectacles, with a bit of white rag on its head like my cap, and cross-sticks for an easel, the others roaring with laughter. That same little imp, Topsy, wanted to know if the flowers I painted faded like other flowers when kept--an unconscious compliment which gained her an extra sixpence when I left. All sorts of races were there--Hottentots, Kafirs, Malays, natives of Namaqualand, and West Africans.

There were fifty ostriches stalking about. Once the old Irishman in charge of them took a holiday for a few days, and when he came back, "Old Cock" was missing, and discovered dead and broken all to bits in his struggles to get himself disentangled from an iron fence. The old man said: "Sure, he had killed himself in more ways than one." The ostriches are most attached couples, and seldom marry again if one of the pair dies. The cock and hen take turns at sitting on the eggs, but many wild eggs are brought in. These are hatched in an incubator in cotton-wool soaked in boiling water, and kept at over 100 degrees of warmth. They take about forty days' hatching. I was lucky enough to be in time to see the gradual entrance into life of the birds. First we heard them chirping inside, then the beak appeared, gradually the whole body worked its way out, the head and neck covered with the most beautiful brown plush, the egg-shaped bodies with a sort of coarse black wool, neither fur nor feathers. The eyes and ears were perfectly active the moment they came out of the shell. The one I painted, half in and half out, turned its head to look at each person who spoke, and seemed to be attending to what we said. After a couple of days in flannel, it was put out in a little paddock, and began eating gravel and other hard morsels with great enjoyment. Their two big toes seem fitted into leather gloves many sizes too large.

The older ones were very amusing to watch, particularly when they first came out in the morning with mincing steps and much waltzing. They had a curious power of flattening themselves out on the ground, with necks and legs stretched out, so that they were quite invisible at a distance among the shrubby plants and dry grass.

The ladies staying at the farm were very Dutch-looking, but Miss D. had quite an English manner, with a gentle voice, notwithstanding her manly strength of character. Everything we ate was made on the farm, as well as a strong wine resembling Madeira. There was a grand vegetable and fruit garden hedged in by a tangle of aloes and geraniums, beliotrope and plumbago. There were two date-palms, pomegranates, loquats, cypresses, blue gums and wattles covered with their golden blossoms, a perfect wood of poplars loaded with the curious hanging nests of sociable finches, and masses of white arums below. Beyond that wood there was not a single tree for miles. One day we all went up to the top of the hill behind the house, 1000 feet of steep climb, where we got a lovely view of the distant sea, and Table Mountain beyond. I found at the top plenty of small starry flowers of various colours, and large yellow thistles, many lovely bulbs, including the pink and white Hypoestes stellata, with eyes as changeable as the peacocks' feathers. One could not tell if they were blue or green, far less paint them. We cooked kabobs, rice, and cakes, and drank strong coffee and wine, close to a muddy pool, which they called a spring. We waited there till the sun got low again. A willow-tree hung over the pool, covered with hanging nests. The pretty yellow builders were very busy over them, and were most entertaining to watch, as they swung their houses in the wind, turning and twisting themselves in and out in all manner of strange attitudes. The cock is said to build many nests before he finds wives to fill them; then the ladies often find fault with the architecture and pull it all to bits for the mere fun of rebuilding it.

One morning we started at seven, in a cart with six horses, Charles D. having come over from his farm (a few miles off) the night before to drive us, with his wife and baby and little black maid. We had a woolly-haired imp to open gates and sit under our feet, while the two pretty nieces rode on horseback. It was both windy and dusty as we floundered on over twenty miles of sand, only losing our way twice. We reached at last a lovely bay of sand and rocks, and a solitary old house and hut, where a large party of cousins were picnicking for a fortnight, running in and out of the sea in the most primitive manner. The house belonged to the family in general, and when no one was there it was locked up and left empty. Two old blacks inhabited the hut, and caught fish enough for all who might come. I wandered off by myself among the rocks and sea-flowers, and found abundance to entertain me. Small red-leaved aloes and dwarf euphorbia, wild olives and geraniums, brown and blue salvias, crassulas, and an endless variety of portulaca and ice-plants (quite exquisite when examined with my magnifying glass), lovely anemones and shells in the rock-pools, with big black birds stalking about on the sands. The family party were disappointed at not seeing me paint, but I was too tired to show off. However, I heard: "She just takes a flower and does it all at once in colours," etc. The hyobanche, both orange and crimson, were gorgeous, and reminded me of the Californian snow-flower. There were lovely balsams of all colours, blue lobelias with pink backs, and masses of large silvery everlastings. The Monsonia spectabilis was also a lovely flower, like a hibiscus, but with an elbow in its stalk a few inches below the flower-bead, which was very remarkable. The droseras too were fine, with flowers of lilac and white as big as a sweet-briar rose: I was told of a scarlet variety, but never found it.

On our return from this expedition we heard one of the valley ostriches had disappeared, no one could make out how. Miss D. said it was hatched from a wild egg, and was led away by its hereditary wandering instincts! They had just finished cutting the feathers of the old ones, pulling stockings over their snake-like heads during the process-- and it was no easy matter to do it; but they cannot kick behind, only in front. I think they seemed all the merrier for losing their beautiful plumes, and waltzed round and round the next morning flapping their wings, with as much grace as any Germans could do. I was never tired of watching these two-legged camels.

Appendix 3: Extracts from: *On the Abuses of Sex: II, Fornication*, in *Essays in Medical Sociology* (1902) by Dr. Elizabeth Blackwell M. D.

One of the first subjects to be investigated by the Christian physiologist is the truth or error of the assertion so widely made, that sexual passion is a much stronger force in men than in women. Very remarkable results have flowed from the attempts to mould society upon this assertion. A simple Christian might reply, "Our religion makes no such distinction; male and female are as one under guidance and judgment of the Divine law." But the physiologist must go farther, and use the light of principles underlying physical truth in order to understand the meaning of facts which arraign and would destroy Christianity.

This mental element of human sex exists in major proportion in the vital force of women, and justifies the statement that the compound faculty of sex is as strong in woman as in man. Those who deny sexual feeling to women, or consider it so light a thing as hardly to be taken into account in social arrangements, confound appetite and passion; they quite lose sight of this immense spiritual force of attraction, which is distinctly human sexual power, and which exists in so very large a proportion in the womanly nature. The impulse towards maternity is an inexorable but beneficent law of woman's nature, and it is a law of sex. The different form which physical sensation necessarily takes in the two sexes, and its intimate connection with and development through the mind (love) in women's nature, serve often to blind even thoughtful and painstaking persons as to the immense power of sexual attraction felt by women. Such one-sided views show a misconception of the meaning of human sex in its entirety. The affectionate husbands of refined women often remark that their wives do not regard the distinctively sexual act with the same intoxicating physical enjoyment that they themselves feel, and they draw the conclusion that the wife possesses no sexual passion. A delicate wife will often confide to her medical adviser (who may be treating her for some special suffering) that at the very time when marriage loves seems to unite them most closely, when her husband's welcome kisses and caresses seem to bring them into profound union, comes an act which mentally separates them, and which may be either indifferent or repugnant to her. But it must be understood that it is not the special act necessary for parentage which is the measure of the compound moral and physical power of sexual passion; it is the profound attraction of one nature to the other which marks passion, and delight in kiss and caress - the love-touch - is physical sexual expression as much as the special act of the male.

It is well known that terror or pain in either sex will temporarily destroy all physical pleasure. In married life, injury from childbirth, or brutal or awkward conjugal approaches, may cause unavoidable shrinking from sexual congress, often wrongly attributed to absence of sexual passion. But the severe and compound suffering experienced by many widows who were strongly attached to their lost partners is also well known to the physician, and this is not simply a mental loss that they feel, but an immense physical deprivation. It is a loss which all the senses suffer by the physical as well as moral void which death has created.

Although physical sexual pleasure is not attached exclusively, or in woman chiefly, to the act of coition, it is also a well-established fact that in healthy loving women, uninjured by the too frequent lesions which result from childbirth, increasing physical satisfaction attaches to the ultimate physical expression of love. A repose and general well-being results from this natural occasional intercourse, whilst the total deprivation of it produces irritability.

On the other hand, the growth in men of the mental element in sexual passion, from mighty wifely love, often comes like a revelation to the husband. The dying words of a man to the wife who, sending away children, friends, every distraction, had bent the whole force of her passionate nature to holding the beloved object in life- -"I never knew before what love meant" - indicates the revelation which the higher element of sexual passion should bring to the lower phase. It is an illustration of the parallelism and natural harmony between the sexes. The prevalent fallacy that sexual passion is the almost exclusive attribute of men, and attached exclusively to the act of coition--a fallacy which exercises so disastrous an effect upon our social arrangements--arises from ignorance of the distinctive character of human sex - viz., its powerful mental element. A tortured girl, done to death by brutal soldiers, may possess a stronger power of human sexual passion than her destroyers.

The comparison so often drawn between the physical development of the comparatively small class of refined and guarded women, and the men of worldly experience whom they marry, is a false comparison. These women have been taught to regard sexual passion as lust and as sin - a sin which it would be a shame for a pure woman to feel, and which she would die rather than confess. She has not been taught that sexual passion is love, even more than lust, and that its ennobling work in humanity is to educate and transfigure the lower by the higher element. The growth and indications of her own nature she is taught to condemn, instead of to respect them as foreshadowing that mighty impulse towards maternity which will place her nearest to the Creator if reverently accepted. . . .

Some medical writers have considered that women are more tyrannically governed than men by the impulses of physical sex. They have dwelt upon the greater proportion of work laid upon women in the reproduction of the race, the prolonged changes and burden of maternity, and the fixed and marked periodical action needed to maintain the aptitude of the physical frame for maternity. They have drawn the conclusion that sex dominates the life of women, and limits them in the power of perfect human growth. This would undoubtedly be the case were sex simply a physical function. The fact in human nature which explains, guides, and should elevate the sexual nature of woman, and mark the beneficence of Creative Force, is this very mental element which distinguishes human from brute sex. This element, gradually expanding under religious teaching and the development of true religious sentiment, becomes the ennobling power of love. Love between the sexes is the highest and mightiest form of human sexual passion. . . .

This power of sex in women is strikingly shown in the enormous influence which they exert upon men for evil. It is not the cold beauty of a statue which enthrals and holds so many men in terrible fascination; it is the living, active power of sexual life embodied in its separate overpowering female phase. The immeasurable depth of degradation into which those women fall, whose sex is thoroughly debased, who have intensified the physical instincts of the brute by the mental power for evil possessed by the human being, indicates the mighty character of sexual power over the nature of woman for corruption. It is also a measure of what the ennobling power of passion may be.

Happily in all civilized countries there is a natural reserve in relation to sexual matters which indicates the reverence with which this high social power of our human nature should be regarded. It is a sign of something wrong in education, or in the social state, when matters which concern the subject of sex are discussed with the same freedom and boldness as other matters. This subject should neither be a topic of idle gossip, of unreserved publicity, nor of cynical display. This natural and beneficial instinct of reserve, springing from unconscious reverence, renders it difficult for one sex to measure and judge the vital power of the other. The independent thought and large observation of each sex is needed in order to arrive at truth. Unhappily, however, women are often falsely instructed by men, for a licentious husband inevitably depraves the sentiment of his wife, because vicious habits have falsified his nature and blinded his perception of the moral law which dominates sexual growth.

Each sex has its own stern battle to fight in resisting temptation, in walking resolutely towards the higher aim of life. It is equally foolish and misleading to attempt to weigh the vital qualities of the sexes, and measure justice and mercy, law and custom, by the supposed results. It is difficult for the child to comprehend that a pound of feathers can weigh as much as a pound of lead. Much of our thought concerning men and women is as rudimentary as the child's. Vast errors of law and custom have arisen in the slow unfolding of human nature from failure to realize the extent of the injury produced by that abuse of sex - fornication. We have not hitherto perceived that, on account of the moral degradation and physical disease which it inevitably produces, lustful trade in the human body is a grave social crime.

In forming a wiser judgement for future guidance, it must be distinctly recognised that the assertion that sexual passion commands more of the vital force of men than of women is a false assertion, based upon a perverted or superficial view of the facts that human nature. Any custom, law, or religious teaching based upon this superficial and essentially false assertion, but necessarily be swept away with the prevalence of sounder physiological views.

A Valentine

What shall I send my sweet today,
  When all the woods attune in love?
  And I would show the lark and dove,
That I can love as well as they.

I'll send a locket full of hair, -
  But no, for it might chance to lie
  Too near her heart, and I should die
Of love's sweet envy to be there.

A violet is sweet to give, -
  Ah, stay! she'd touch it with her lips,
  And, after such complete eclipse,
How could my soul consent to live?

I'll send a kiss, for that would be
  The quickest sent, the lightest borne,
  And well I know tomorrow morn
She'll send it back again to me.

Go, happy winds; ah, do not stay,
  Enamoured of my lady's cheek,
  But hasten home, and I'll bespeak
Your services another day!

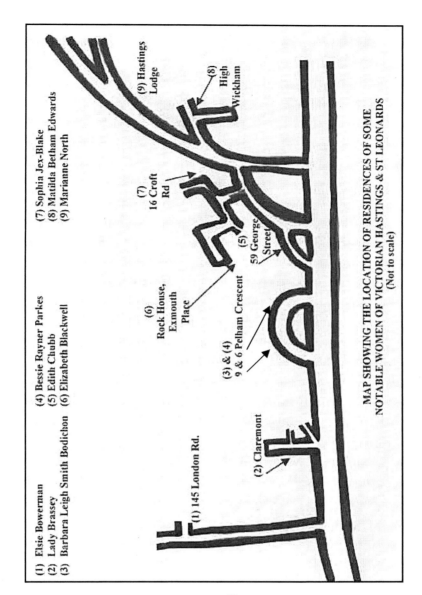

(1) Elsie Bowerman
(2) Lady Brassey
(3) Barbara Leigh Smith Bodichon

(4) Bessie Rayner Parkes
(5) Edith Chubb
(6) Elizabeth Blackwell

(7) Sophia Jex-Blake
(8) Matilda Betham Edwards
(9) Marianne North

(1) 145 London Rd.

(2) Claremont

(3) & (4) 9 & 6 Pelham Crescent

(6) Rock House, Exmouth Place

(5) 59 George Street

(7) 16 Croft Rd

(8) High Wickham

(9) Hastings Lodge

MAP SHOWING THE LOCATION OF RESIDENCES OF SOME
NOTABLE WOMEN OF VICTORIAN HASTINGS & ST LEONARDS
(Not to scale)